ELEANOR
OF
AQUITAINE

ELEANOR
OF
AQUITAINE

Zoë Coralnik Kaplan

1987
CHELSEA HOUSE PUBLISHERS
NEW YORK
NEW HAVEN   PHILADELPHIA

PROJECT EDITOR: John W. Selfridge
ASSOCIATE EDITOR: Marian W. Taylor
EDITORIAL COORDINATOR: Karyn Gullen Browne
EDITORIAL STAFF: Maria Behan
    Pierre Hauser
    Perry Scott King
    Kathleen McDermott
    Howard Ratner
    Alma Rodriguez-Sokol
    Bert Yaeger
LAYOUT: Irene Friedman
ART ASSISTANTS: Noreen Lamb
    Carol McDougall
    Victoria Tomaselli
COVER ILLUSTRATION: Peter McCaffrey
PICTURE RESEARCH: Diane Wallace

Frontispiece courtesy of Art Resource

First Printing

Library of Congress Cataloging in Publication Data

Kaplan, Zoë. ELEANOR OF AQUITAINE.

(World leaders past & present)
Bibliography: p.
Includes index.
    1. Eleanor, Queen, consort of Henry II, King of England,
1122?–1204—Juvenile literature. 2. Great Britain—Queens—
Biography—Juvenile literature. 3. France—Queens—Biography—
Juvenile literature. [1. Eleanor, Queen, consort of Henry II, King of
England, 1122?–1204. 2. Kings, queens, rulers, etc.]
I. Title. II. Series.
DA209.E6K37   1986   942.03′1′0924 [B] [92]   86-13689

ISBN 0-87754-552-7

Contents

ADENAUER
ALEXANDER THE GREAT
MARC ANTONY
KING ARTHUR
ATATÜRK
ATTLEE
BEGIN
BEN-GURION
BISMARCK
LÉON BLUM
BOLÍVAR
CESARE BORGIA
BRANDT
BREZHNEV
CAESAR
CALVIN
CASTRO
CATHERINE THE GREAT
CHARLEMAGNE
CHIANG KAI-SHEK
CHURCHILL
CLEMENCEAU
CLEOPATRA
CORTÉS
CROMWELL
DANTON
DE GAULLE
DE VALERA
DISRAELI
EISENHOWER
ELEANOR OF AQUITAINE
QUEEN ELIZABETH I
FERDINAND AND ISABELLA
FRANCO

FREDERICK THE GREAT
INDIRA GANDHI
MOHANDAS GANDHI
GARIBALDI
GENGHIS KHAN
GLADSTONE
GORBACHEV
HAMMARSKJÖLD
HENRY VIII
HENRY OF NAVARRE
HINDENBURG
HITLER
HO CHI MINH
HUSSEIN
IVAN THE TERRIBLE
ANDREW JACKSON
JEFFERSON
JOAN OF ARC
POPE JOHN XXIII
LYNDON JOHNSON
JUÁREZ
JOHN F. KENNEDY
KENYATTA
KHOMEINI
KHRUSHCHEV
MARTIN LUTHER KING, JR.
KISSINGER
LENIN
LINCOLN
LLOYD GEORGE
LOUIS XIV
LUTHER
JUDAS MACCABEUS
MAO ZEDONG

MARY, QUEEN OF SCOTS
GOLDA MEIR
METTERNICH
MUSSOLINI
NAPOLEON
NASSER
NEHRU
NERO
NICHOLAS II
NIXON
NKRUMAH
PERICLES
PERÓN
QADDAFI
ROBESPIERRE
ELEANOR ROOSEVELT
FRANKLIN D. ROOSEVELT
THEODORE ROOSEVELT
SADAT
STALIN
SUN YAT-SEN
TAMERLANE
THATCHER
TITO
TROTSKY
TRUDEAU
TRUMAN
VICTORIA
WASHINGTON
WEIZMANN
WOODROW WILSON
XERXES
ZHOU ENLAI

ON LEADERSHIP
Arthur M. Schlesinger, jr.

LEADERSHIP, it may be said, is really what makes the world go round. Love no doubt smooths the passage; but love is a private transaction between consenting adults. Leadership is a public transaction with history. The idea of leadership affirms the capacity of individuals to move, inspire, and mobilize masses of people so that they act together in pursuit of an end. Sometimes leadership serves good purposes, sometimes bad; but whether the end is benign or evil, great leaders are those men and women who leave their personal stamp on history.

Now, the very concept of leadership implies the proposition that individuals can make a difference. This proposition has never been universally accepted. From classical times to the present day, eminent thinkers have regarded individuals as no more than the agents and pawns of larger forces, whether the gods and goddesses of the ancient world or, in the modern era, race, class, nation, the dialectic, the will of the people, the spirit of the times, history itself. Against such forces, the individual dwindles into insignificance.

So contends the thesis of historical determinism. Tolstoy's great novel *War and Peace* offers a famous statement of the case. Why, Tolstoy asked, did millions of men in the Napoleonic wars, denying their human feelings and their common sense, move back and forth across Europe slaughtering their fellows? "The war," Tolstoy answered, "was bound to happen simply because it was bound to happen." All prior history predetermined it. As for leaders, they, Tolstoy said, "are but the labels that serve to give a name to an end and, like labels, they have the least possible connection with the event." The greater the leader, "the more conspicuous the inevitability and the predestination of every act he commits." The leader, said Tolstoy, is "the slave of history."

Determinism takes many forms. Marxism is the determinism of class. Nazism the determinism of race. But the idea of men and women as the slaves of history runs athwart the deepest human instincts. Rigid determinism abolishes the idea of human freedom—

the assumption of free choice that underlies every move we make, every word we speak, every thought we think. It abolishes the idea of human responsibility, since it is manifestly unfair to reward or punish people for actions that are by definition beyond their control. No one can live consistently by any deterministic creed. The Marxist states prove this themselves by their extreme susceptibility to the cult of leadership.

More than that, history refutes the idea that individuals make no difference. In December 1931 a British politician crossing Park Avenue in New York City between 76th and 77th Streets around 10:30 P.M. looked in the wrong direction and was knocked down by an automobile—a moment, he later recalled, of a man aghast, a world aglare: "I do not understand why I was not broken like an eggshell or squashed like a gooseberry." Fourteen months later an American politician, sitting in an open car in Miami, Florida, was fired on by an assassin; the man beside him was hit. Those who believe that individuals make no difference to history might well ponder whether the next two decades would have been the same had Mario Constasino's car killed Winston Churchill in 1931 and Giuseppe Zangara's bullet killed Franklin Roosevelt in 1933. Suppose, in addition, that Adolf Hitler had been killed in the street fighting during the Munich *Putsch* of 1923 and that Lenin had died of typhus during World War I. What would the 20th century be like now?

For better or for worse, individuals do make a difference. "The notion that a people can run itself and its affairs anonymously," wrote the philosopher William James, "is now well known to be the silliest of absurdities. Mankind does nothing save through initiatives on the part of inventors, great or small, and imitation by the rest of us—these are the sole factors in human progress. Individuals of genius show the way, and set the patterns, which common people then adopt and follow."

Leadership, James suggests, means leadership in thought as well as in action. In the long run, leaders in thought may well make the greater difference to the world. But, as Woodrow Wilson once said, "Those only are leaders of men, in the general eye, who lead in action. . . . It is at their hands that new thought gets its translation into the crude language of deeds." Leaders in thought often invent in solitude and obscurity, leaving to later generations the tasks of imitation. Leaders in action—the leaders portrayed in this series—have to be effective in their own time.

And they cannot be effective by themselves. They must act in response to the rhythms of their age. Their genius must be adapted, in a phrase of William James's, "to the receptivities of the moment." Leaders are useless without followers. "There goes the mob," said the French politician hearing a clamor in the streets. "I am their leader. I must follow them." Great leaders turn the inchoate emotions of the mob to purposes of their own. They seize on the opportunities of their time, the hopes, fears, frustrations, crises, potentialities. They succeed when events have prepared the way for them, when the community is awaiting to be aroused, when they can provide the clarifying and organizing ideas. Leadership ignites the circuit between the individual and the mass and thereby alters history.

It may alter history for better or for worse. Leaders have been responsible for the most extravagant follies and most monstrous crimes that have beset suffering humanity. They have also been vital in such gains as humanity has made in individual freedom, religious and racial tolerance, social justice and respect for human rights.

There is no sure way to tell in advance who is going to lead for good and who for evil. But a glance at the gallery of men and women in *World Leaders—Past and Present* suggests some useful tests.

One test is this: do leaders lead by force or by persuasion? By command or by consent? Through most of history leadership was exercised by the divine right of authority. The duty of followers was to defer and to obey. "Theirs not to reason why,/ Theirs but to do and die." On occasion, as with the so-called "enlightened despots" of the 18th century in Europe, absolutist leadership was animated by humane purposes. More often, absolutism nourished the passion for domination, land, gold and conquest and resulted in tyranny.

The great revolution of modern times has been the revolution of equality. The idea that all people should be equal in their legal condition has undermined the old structure of authority, hierarchy and deference. The revolution of equality has had two contrary effects on the nature of leadership. For equality, as Alexis de Tocqueville pointed out in his great study *Democracy in America*, might mean equality in servitude as well as equality in freedom.

"I know of only two methods of establishing equality in the political world," Tocqueville wrote. "Rights must be given to every citizen, or none at all to anyone . . . save one, who is the master of all." There was no middle ground "between the sovereignty of all and the absolute power of one man." In his astonishing prediction of 20th-century totalitarian dictatorship, Tocqueville explained how the revolution of equality could lead to the *"Führerprinzip"* and more terrible absolutism than the world had ever known.

But when rights are given to every citizen and the sovereignty of all is established, the problem of leadership takes a new form, becomes more exacting than ever before. It is easy to issue commands and enforce them by the rope and the stake, the concentration camp and the *gulag.* It is much harder to use argument and achievement to overcome opposition and win consent. The Founding Fathers of the United States understood the difficulty. They believed that history had given them the opportunity to decide, as Alexander Hamilton wrote in the first Federalist Paper, whether men are indeed capable of basing government on "reflection and choice, or whether they are forever destined to depend . . . on accident and force."

Government by reflection and choice called for a new style of leadership and a new quality of followership. It required leaders to be responsive to popular concerns, and it required followers to be active and informed participants in the process. Democracy does not eliminate emotion from politics; sometimes it fosters demagoguery; but it is confident that, as the greatest of democratic leaders put it, you cannot fool all of the people all of the time. It measures leadership by results and retires those who overreach or falter or fail.

It is true that in the long run despots are measured by results too. But they can postpone the day of judgment, sometimes indefinitely, and in the meantime they can do infinite harm. It is also true that democracy is no guarantee of virtue and intelligence in government, for the voice of the people is not necessarily the voice of God. But democracy, by assuring the right of opposition, offers built-in resistance to the evils inherent in absolutism. As the theologian Reinhold Niebuhr summed it up, "Man's capacity for justice makes democracy possible, but man's inclination to injustice makes democracy necessary."

A second test for leadership is the end for which power is sought. When leaders have as their goal the supremacy of a master race or the promotion of totalitarian revolution or the acquisition and exploitation of colonies or the protection of greed and privilege or the preservation of personal power, it is likely that their leadership will do little to advance the cause of humanity. When their goal is the abolition of slavery, the liberation of women, the enlargement of opportunity for the poor and powerless, the extension of equal rights to racial minorities, the defense of the freedoms of expression and opposition, it is likely that their leadership will increase the sum of human liberty and welfare.

Leaders have done great harm to the world. They have also conferred great benefits. You will find both sorts in this series. Even "good" leaders must be regarded with a certain wariness. Leaders are not demigods; they put on their trousers one leg after another just like ordinary mortals. No leader is infallible, and every leader needs to be reminded of this at regular intervals. Irreverence irritates leaders but is their salvation. Unquestioning submission corrupts leaders and demands followers. Making a cult of a leader is always a mistake. Fortunately hero worship generates its own antidote. "Every hero," said Emerson, "becomes a bore at last."

The signal benefit the great leaders confer is to embolden the rest of us to live according to our own best selves, to be active, insistent, and resolute in affirming our own sense of things. For great leaders attest to the reality of human freedom against the supposed inevitabilities of history. And they attest to the wisdom and power that may lie within the most unlikely of us, which is why Abraham Lincoln remains the supreme example of great leadership. A great leader, said Emerson, exhibits new possibilities to all humanity. "We feed on genius. . . . Great men exist that there may be greater men."

Great leaders, in short, justify themselves by emancipating and empowering their followers. So humanity struggles to master its destiny, remembering with Alexis de Tocqueville: "It is true that around every man a fatal circle is traced beyond which he cannot pass; but within the wide verge of that circle he is powerful and free; as it is with man, so with communities."

—*New York*

1
The Source

On an October day in 1149, Eleanor, queen of France, knelt at the feet of Pope Eugenius III, the leader of the Roman Catholic church, and asked to be granted a divorce from her husband, Louis VII. After a long and dangerous sea voyage, on which her ship had been lost for months and almost wrecked, the queen had just landed in Italy from faraway Jerusalem, where she had accompanied King Louis on a crusade — a type of military campaign waged by Christian kings of the time against the Muslim Turks. (The Christians called these Turks "infidels," meaning those who did not conform to Christianity, and such war was considered a holy enterprise by the Christians of medieval Europe.) Queen Eleanor counted on her beauty and her persuasive personality to persuade the pope.

Though a great deal was allowed the rich and powerful in 12th-century Catholic Europe, divorce was practically impossible for any prince or nobleman. A woman, regardless of social class, did not share many of her brothers' or husband's privileges. The lower classes had no personal or individual rights at all, being kept in servitude to their masters, both spiritual and secular, under a system called feu-

GIRAUDON/ART RESOURCE

This rock-crystal and pearl vase was given by Eleanor to Louis VII as a wedding present. Now part of the Louvre in Paris, it is the sole possession of Eleanor's that has survived to this day.

Godfrey of Bouillon, French leader of the First Crusade (1095–99). During the 12th century, several members of the family of Eleanor of Aquitaine (c.1122–1204) became deeply involved in these expeditions to "free" the Holy Land of domination by the "infidels," as the European Christians termed the Muslims. Eleanor herself would witness the disastrous Second Crusade.

dalism. Eleanor, an independent spirit despite her technical status as her husband's property, asserted herself by attempting to take charge of her own life and interests.

Using all her powers of logic, as well as her feminine charm, Eleanor tried to win the pope's consent to a divorce. Louis, apparently, did not share her wish to separate, and since such a marriage was primarily a political rather than a private matter, the pope, after listening patiently to this extraordinary request, kindly but firmly commanded the royal couple to reconcile their differences. Answering all of the queen's most powerful arguments with authoritative skill based on the teachings of the

Departure of soldiers for battle during the Second Crusade (1147–49). Historians generally call the Crusades "one of the great lost causes of history" for failing to dislodge the Muslims from the Holy Land. However, Europeans were greatly influenced by their contact with Middle Eastern culture.

Church, Pope Eugenius sent Eleanor back to France with Louis, and her wish was overruled, if only for the time being.

Whatever her feelings may have been, the following year in Paris Eleanor gave birth to a second daughter, only her second child in 13 years of marriage. Since it seemed unlikely that Eleanor would produce a son and heir, Louis reluctantly gave in to Eleanor's unchanged wishes. (His advisers had convinced him that only through another marriage could France hope for a prince.) Thus, in 1152, three years after her confrontation with the pope, the queen not only gained her divorce — the pope's consent having been obtained — but proceeded, astonishingly, to marry into another royal house. Her new husband was the young and powerful Henry Plantagenet, duke of Normandy and count of Anjou, soon to be King Henry II of England, with whom she would found a dynasty that would shape and change the history of Europe. It is, however, in her own right as a personality and influence that she is best remembered. As historian Marion Meade says in her book *Eleanor of Aquitaine: A Biography,* "Despite her association with . . . four kings [her two husbands, Louis VII of France and Henry II of England, and her sons Richard the Lion-Hearted and John], she struggled to retain her own identity, and it is a measure of her success that years after her death she survives not as Queen Eleanor of England or Queen Eleanor of France but simply as Eleanor of Aquitaine."

Who was Eleanor of Aquitaine that she was able, in a totally male-dominated world, to retain such control over her own life? There are several factors which, in combination, help to explain her unique impact on her times. Her beauty was legendary, her charm and intelligence universally acclaimed. In an era when most people, however nobly born, were illiterate, her highly developed understanding of literature and poetry — an important part of her heritage — was unusual. Her energy and freedom of movement — she traveled with kings and warriors as an equal throughout Europe and the Middle East — were unparalleled. Her comprehension of

> *Eleanor belonged to a race of troubadours and warriors.*
> —RICHARD BARBER
> British historian

Louis VII, also known as Louis the Young, ruled France from 1137 until his death in 1180. He was the first of four kings in the life of Eleanor of Aquitaine — their marriage was dissolved in 1152 after the couple failed to produce a son to inherit the throne.

THE BETTMANN ARCHIVE

and participation in the European politics of the day were exceptional. Eleanor has been called the key political figure of the 12th century, a century in which politics were just as complex as they are today. To understand this remarkable woman and the impression she made on her world, the special circumstances of her heritage and upbringing have to be considered.

Born in 1122 in the duchy of Aquitaine, a cultural center in southern France, Eleanor was the daughter of Duke William X, a spirited man, whose vast domains covered a quarter of what would now be France. Including such important cities as Tours, Poitiers, and Bordeaux, his lands stretched from the Loire River in the north to the base of the Pyrenees mountains in the south, from the eastern province of Auvergne to the Atlantic Ocean in the west. William traced his lineage back three centuries to William I, duke of Aquitaine and count of Poitou — still another part of the family's huge holdings.

Influential as Eleanor's father was in her development, even more so was her grandfather, Duke William IX — known as the "Troubadour," or poet and singer — whose court has been described as the center of western European culture of that period. Young Eleanor's basic character was formed during long summer evenings she spent in the great hall of the palace in Poitiers, capital of their county of Poitou and her main childhood home. She was allowed to sit up late, surrounded by musicians, acrobats, and storytellers, and soon grew accustomed to the social graces and cultivated talk of her elders. In Poitiers, the child lived a life of elegance and sophistication, which — together with her good health, strong will, and high spirits — gave her a most advantageous beginning.

Nor was she only fortunate in her surroundings and robust constitution. Contemporary accounts always speak of Eleanor as a great beauty and give the impression that she was probably blond, with large, light eyes, a straight nose, fair skin, good teeth, and a slender figure. Both her open nature and quick wit were appreciated and encouraged at her father's court. She also possessed a sharp in-

THE BETTMANN ARCHIVE

Henry II became king of England in 1154. Eleanor's marriage to Henry Plantagenet just two months after her divorce from Louis VII was a political disaster for the French king — the addition of Aquitaine to Henry's Angevin lands constituted a major threat to Louis's plans for the expansion of his Capetian kingdom.

telligence and an interest in learning. In an age when intellectual interests were the exception rather than the rule, Eleanor stood out in her pleasure in acquiring knowledge. Hers was an extraordinary combination of good luck and a fine understanding of how to make the most of it, a trait that would continue to benefit her throughout her long, eventful life.

When Eleanor was only four years old, her father had become duke upon the death of William IX. When she was eight, both her gentle young mother, Aénor, and her younger brother William Aigret, the heir to the duchy, died. Her mother's softer presence gone, Eleanor was now completely under the influence of her temperamental father and her free-spirited maternal grandmother, from whom many of her

This 15th-century engraving from Germany depicts life in a knight's castle. Eleanor's devotion to literature, poetry, music, and learning made a marked impression on her contemporaries and is an important part of her legacy.

ideas of independent behavior came. The only other child in the family was a slightly younger sister, Petronilla. Despite grumblings about her being a female, Eleanor became the heir apparent of her father's lands.

As heir, she would accompany Duke William X on his "progresses" or tours, which members of the nobility undertook periodically to see to various business matters concerning their lands and holdings. Legal problems involving his subjects had to be heard and judged by the ruler, and in a time when there were constant skirmishes between rival nobles, homage — a ceremonial declaration of loyalty — was due to the duke as the overlord and protector of his vassals, those lesser lords of the duchy bound to him by vows of allegiance. (Duke William, in turn, was the vassal of the king of France, his overlord.) Politics were mixed with lavish entertainments by the lord of each castle that William and his daughter visited, as one lord tried to outdo the other for the ducal favor. It was undoubtedly on these progresses, which ranged from Poitiers to Bordeaux to Toulouse, that Eleanor, a quick and observant girl, began to gain her first understanding of administration and statecraft.

Despite the richness of Aquitaine's soil and the mildness of its climate, it would be a mistake to think that most of its inhabitants lived well or better than people elsewhere. The realities of life that were the lot of the poor, hard-working, insecure peasants, whose huts lay outside the walls of the great

A medieval game of checkers. Unlike most women of her time, Eleanor grew up in an intellectually stimulating atmosphere — surrounded by storytellers, poets, and cultivated people of the Aquitaine court — to become a highly intelligent woman with a rich cultural appetite.

SNARK/ART RESOURCE

fortress castles and palaces, were harsh in spite of the favorable conditions that nature had provided. Their very survival depended on the goodwill of their lords. Under the feudal system — the political, social, and economic structure widespread in Europe throughout the Middle Ages — peasants were obligated to give their masters a good part of the crops they harvested, leaving little for themselves.

Even though Eleanor must have had some idea of the conditions of life outside her own experience, it was a splendid life that surrounded her. It was the brilliant court of Aquitaine that made the other French say that the Aquitainians "lived for pleasure." The tradition of poetry that had begun with Eleanor's grandfather would flower in the time of his granddaughter into the tradition that came to be called "courtly love," which idealized women.

The Church had looked with disfavor on William the Troubadour's interest in poetry and women. Like his father, Duke William X got into trouble, though for different reasons, and was finally excommunicated. This was the most severe punishment that could be given by the Church, as it deprived an individual of his or her rights of church membership. The excommunication, which took place in 1135, when Eleanor was 13 years old, occurred because Duke William supported the French candidate for pope in a papal dispute in which the Italian pope was backed by most of the powerful princes and churchmen of his time. (In medieval times, even more than now, the Catholic church played an important role in world politics.) Although the stubborn, temperamental duke continued his support of the so-called "antipope" and led many battles on his behalf, he began to be increasingly worried by his situation, and by 1137 wanted to be reconciled to the Church. Accordingly, in the early spring of that year, he decided to go on a pilgrimage, a commonplace occurrence in the Middle Ages, to atone for his sins at the shrine of Saint James at Santiago de Compostela in Spain. On the way, while crossing the Pyrenees mountains, which separate France from Spain, he developed a fever from some polluted water and died. In April 1137 the 15-year-old

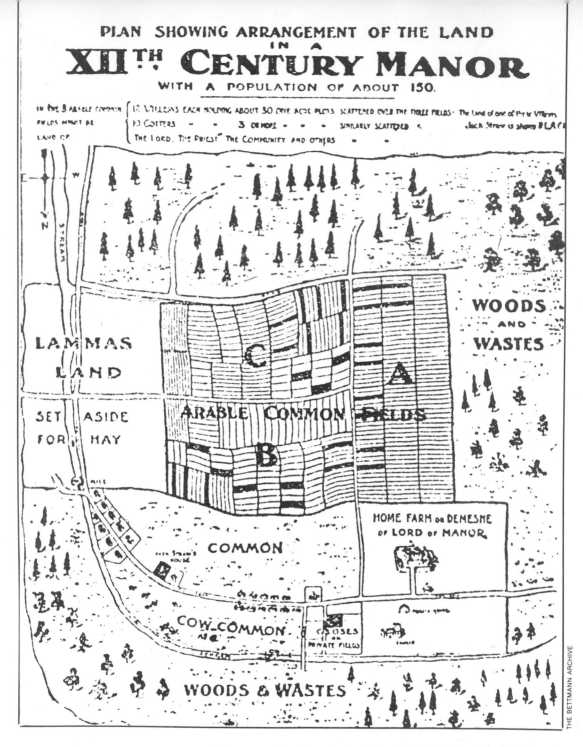

PLAN SHOWING ARRANGEMENT OF THE LAND
IN A
XIITH CENTURY MANOR
WITH A POPULATION OF ABOUT 150.

Diagram showing typical land distribution in 12th-century feudal society. While Eleanor experienced the affluent life of the French court, outside the walls of her family's castles most peasants lived extremely difficult lives and remained dependent on the nobility for protection.

Eleanor became the powerful duchess of Aquitaine.

Knowing the kind of legacy, political and military, that he was leaving his daughter, William wrote a will in which he placed her, together with his possessions, under the protection of King Louis VI of France. On his deathbed, the duke showed a better understanding of political realities than he ever had before. In William's last will and testament Meade states that he bequeathed "to his beloved daughter Eleanor, his sole heir . . . his fief [or dukedom]. . . . To his overlord, the king of France, he bestowed both his domains and his daughter, in the hope that the worthy Louis would guard both treasures until he found the new duchess a suitable husband. . . . In the meantime, the king had the right to enjoy the use of Eleanor's lands."

The dying William X could not have envisioned the immediate results of his will. He could not have dreamed that within three months his Eleanor would be the wife of the crown prince of France, and that by midsummer of that year, 1137, the old king would be dead and she would have become not only countess of Poitou and duchess of Aquitaine but queen of France.

Louis VI, also known as Louis the Fat, king of France. When Eleanor's father, Duke William X of Aquitaine, died in 1137, he bequeathed her — and his duchy — to his overlord, Louis VI. Within months, Eleanor had married the French king's son, the crown prince Louis, and shortly thereafter became queen of France.

2

Queen of France

Paris in the middle of the 12th century was already a very old, very crowded city, built on Roman ruins and centered on a small island in the Seine River. This island — now called the *Île de la Cité* — was dominated by the old, heavily fortified castle of the king at one end and the properties belonging to the archbishop at the other. Stone bridges connected the *Île* with the *faubourgs*, or suburbs, rapidly spreading beyond the banks of the river.

At this time, the French capital was not only growing fast as a center of commerce on the right bank of the river, but a "refuge for philosophy" was being established amidst the pleasant woods and meadows of the left bank of the Seine. Here celebrated French thinkers lectured and presented fresh views on traditional religious and philosophical matters. Perhaps the most famous of these scholars was Peter Abelard, who was leading new challenges to the Church's doctrines. Abelard believed that questions of religion were open to debate using reason; one did not have to accept church tenets merely on faith. Church leaders, alarmed at this threat to their authority, rose to combat Abelard's influence. They denounced the philosopher's teachings as heretical

How apt art thou, O Paris, to bewitch and seduce!
—PIERRE DE LA CELLE
one of the masters of philosophy in 12th-century Paris

Peter Abelard, controversial French theologian and philosopher, discusses morality with his disciples. At the time of Eleanor's arrival in Paris as queen in 1137, Abelard was leading a challenge to traditional church teachings by advocating the use of reason in matters of faith.

Like so many political marriages, no account was taken of the temperaments of the pair.

—RICHARD BARBER
British historian, on
Eleanor and Louis'
marriage

GIRAUDON/ART RESOURCE

The west façade of the great cathedral in Chartres, France. This 12th-century structure is considered a fine example of Gothic cathedral architecture. The pointed arches, rib vaults, and lofty spires of the new style reflected the intense religious aspirations of the age.

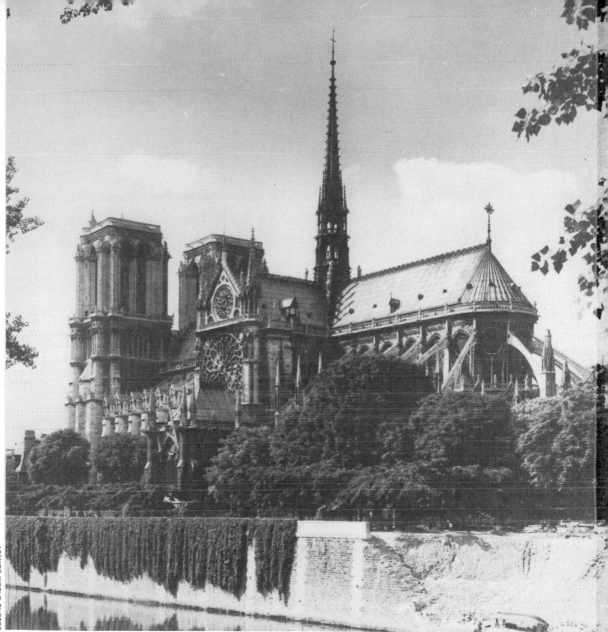

and eventually forced him into exile.

But the issues Abelard raised remained, and the intellectual atmosphere he helped promote encouraged others to seek further knowledge. Young scholars from near and far flocked to Paris to take part in the city's unrestricted atmosphere, one in which they could share ideas as well as enjoy themselves in more worldly ways. It was into this place of intense life, this atmosphere of brilliant ideas flourishing among narrow streets and rickety houses,

Rear view of the Cathedral of Nôtre Dame on the Île de la Cité in Paris. Another Gothic masterpiece, Nôtre Dame today dominates the island in the Seine River where the city of Paris was first established and where Eleanor resided as queen.

27

A 14th-century manuscript of *The Romance of the Rose*, a popular allegorical poem from the Middle Ages, contains an illustration depicting Abelard and his wife, Heloise. Abelard's ideas were part of the freewheeling intellectual atmosphere that pervaded Paris as Eleanor and Louis began their rule.

that Eleanor came as a 15-year-old bride.

The gloomy and formal palace of the Capets (the family name of the French kings) was a sharp contrast to the sunshine and silks, the unguarded speech and comparative freedom of movement the young girl was used to. It was as much a contrast as the harsher language of the north was to her own musical southern speech. It was as much a contrast as that between the personalities of Louis and Eleanor themselves.

The two could not have been more different in temperament or outlook on life. The young king was extremely religious and quiet, unused to and uninterested in society. Had his older brother Philip, the heir to the French throne, not died in an accident, it was said that Louis would gladly have shut himself away from worldly concerns and become a monk. He was an unlikely match for the sophisticated, fun-loving, extravagant, and extremely sociable young queen; nor were his Parisian courtiers any more elegant or well-mannered than their king. So it was that in spite of the elaborate parties and entertainments she gave, Eleanor found the royal court in her new capital as boring and uninspiring as she found her new husband.

Louis however, did not share Eleanor's displea-

It is only in contrast to her husband Louis that [Eleanor] might fairly be called wanton: for Louis' gentle and pious nature was more suited to the religious than to the royal life.
—RICHARD BARBER
British historian

28

sure. The chronicles of the time make it clear that whatever her feelings, for him theirs was a loving as well as a politically advantageous alliance. The young king raised no objection when his glamorous wife spent tremendous amounts of money on jewels, elegant clothes, and parties. Much later, when Eleanor sought a divorce, Louis did not agree to it at first, even though she had not provided him with the most important reason for a royal marriage, namely a son and heir to the throne. Clearly, Louis wanted to make her happy and it was his tragedy that he was unable to do so.

By virtue of her background, Eleanor was better equipped to rule than was Louis. Their first disagreement over matters of state arose when the cit-

An illustration from a medieval manuscript on the ethics of Aristotle, with the six ladies representing the cardinal religious virtues. Eleanor knew Latin fluently, and was said to be familiar with Aristotelian logic, a most unusual accomplishment for a woman of the 12th century.

The abbey of Fontenay, a 12th-century cloister. King Louis VII was originally interested in the sheltered life of a monk until the accidental death of his older brother made him heir to the throne. Eleanor, a more worldly sort, could never quite relate to the pious side of Louis's personality.

izens of Poitiers rebelled against the royal couple shortly after their marriage in 1137, and declared themselves a free city. According to Meade, they did not want to be under the rule of "a foreign king merely because their land happened to be part of his wife's real estate." Louis brutally suppressed the uprising in order to look powerful in the eyes of Eleanor and the world. He then demanded that the children of the town's leading citizens be sent as hostages into his own kingdom. Only the interference of the powerful Abbé Suger, his own priest and the most trusted adviser of his late father, King Louis VI, made the young king change his mind and let the hostages go free. This incident left a negative impression on Eleanor. She thought her husband too harsh at one extreme and too easily led at the other. Eleanor lacked not only love but respect for Louis, a tragic combination, even though the marriage was a state affair, where personal feelings were considered secondary.

Although she was depressed and lonely since neither her husband nor French society were to her

GIRAUDON/ART RESOURCE

SVGERIVS ABS

liking, historians think that some of the intellectually stimulating ideas that filled Paris at the time were not lost on the young queen. Many have pointed out that her sharp reasoning skills and her ability to influence others may have resulted from her exposure to the new ways of thinking prevalent in Paris.

In 1141 a serious political-religious conflict arose between the young king and Pope Innocent II in Rome. When an important church post in the French city of Bourges became vacant, Louis himself appointed a bishop to fill it. Meanwhile, the pope

A stained glass window from the Church of Saint Denis portrays Abbé Suger, a prominent religious figure and adviser to both Louis VI and Louis the Young. Abbé Suger's administrative talents prompted Louis VII to appoint him regent of his kingdom while the king was absent during the Second Crusade.

A page from the notebook of Abbé (later Saint) Bernard of Clairvaux called *St. Bernard on the twelve degrees of humility*. The powerful Bernard thought Abelard's progressive teachings to be the work of Satan and led a successful campaign to have his "heresies" silenced.

had appointed another bishop and sent him to Bourges to take up his new duties. Louis refused to allow interference with his choice, and the result was that this most devout of men was excommunicated. Although this excommunication was lifted after the pope died two years later and the new pope, Eugenius III, wanted to make peace with France, the experience had a lasting effect on Louis, making him even more pious than he had been before. Eleanor, it is said, was not overly concerned with these matters during this crucial period for her husband. Instead, she concentrated her considerable energies on becoming a royal mother as well as intriguing to bring about the marriage of her only sister, Petronilla.

In 1145, at the then advanced age of 23, Eleanor gave birth to her long-awaited first child. This child was not the son necessary to inherit the throne, but a daughter named Marie, who was one day to become an influential figure in her own right. She would become very much her mother's daughter.

THE METROPOLITAN MUSEUM OF ART

A French ivory seal matrix from the 12th century shows an abbot with his crosier, or staff. Bernard of Clairvaux, say some historians, held Eleanor in disdain because of her lavish, secular lifestyle and the effect he thought it was having on the pious King Louis VII.

3

Going to Jerusalem

The year 1145 was not only marked by the birth of Eleanor and Louis's first daughter, but also by the pope's call for a new crusade against the Muslim Turks. In December 1144 the Turks had captured the important Christian city of Edessa in the Holy Land and were threatening other cities. These cities, in the so-called "Latin Kingdom," which included Syria and Palestine, were under the rule of mostly French Christian princes, descendants of the conquering Europeans of the First Crusade, which had been waged over a half-century before. The purpose of the Turks' attack was to drive the enemy Christians out of what the Muslims considered their own territory. This territory included Jerusalem, the sacred city of the three Western faiths: Judaism, Christianity, and Islam.

Pope Eugenius's choice of Louis to lead what came to be known as the Second Crusade was mainly political. Since most of the European rulers of the lands in the Middle East were from the provinces of France, it was Louis, their king and feudal overlord, to whom they owed honor and support. The French had the most to lose in overseas possessions, but it was Louis's deeply religious nature that stirred the

Anyone seeing these cohorts with their helmets and bucklers shining in the sun, with their banners streaming in the breeze, would have been certain that they were about to triumph over all the enemies of the cross and reduce to submission all the countries of the Orient.

—contemporary account of the Second Crusade

Knights of the First Crusade fight to liberate Jerusalem from the Muslims. The 1144 fall of Edessa, one of the Latin states established during the First Crusade, greatly dismayed the West. Pope Eugenius III raised the call for a second crusade, but in contrast to the previous expedition, this venture would be led by kings — Louis VII of France and Conrad III of Germany. The Crusaders hoped to strengthen the defenses of Jerusalem, the city most revered by Christians.

king of France to want to lead a crusade. Only by enduring all the hardships and sufferings that would be part of the long, difficult, and dangerous journey to the Middle East, to say nothing of the bloody battles that would have to be fought there to save the holy places of the Christian faith from the "infidels," would Louis feel he had really atoned for his sins and made his peace with God.

Interestingly, while it was Louis's spirit that was suited to such a venture, it was Eleanor's family that had already won fame in this sphere. Her soldier-poet grandfather, William IX, duke of Aquitaine and count of Poitou, had been one of the leaders of the First Crusade in the last part of the 11th century. When Eleanor encouraged her Aquitainian lords to pledge their lands and their lives for the sake of the Holy Land, they were not overly eager to do so. Many recalled the sacrifice of life and the enormous draining of their wealth such an enterprise entailed. A lot of discussion and disagreement about how to proceed — in raising money, training an army, making travel arrangements — ensued for months in both noble and religious circles. Then, on Easter Sunday 1146, the renowned churchman Bernard of Clairvaux delivered a sermon encouraging people to join the crusade. His powerful personality inspired the thousands of nobles and commoners who had come from near and far to hear him. After stressing that the pope had promised absolution — or forgiveness of sins — to anyone who would go on the dangerous journey and fight in a "holy war," Bernard apparently cast a spell with his famous speech-making skills. A great wave of approval was heard and many of those present expressed their eagerness to join the holy cause.

Queen Eleanor, together with many other noble-women, made preparations to go along on the hard and dangerous journey. Although the pope had expressly forbidden luxury on the crusade, historians tell us that Eleanor and some other women filled many wagons with trunks of clothes, furs, jewels, cosmetics, soft bedding, towels, soap, cookware, fine glasses, and even carpets. Others on the crusade considered all this excessive, especially in light

> *He has never gone against the enemy without having received the Sacrament, and at his return he recites vespers and compline. God is the Alpha and Omega of his enterprise.*
> —member of the Second Crusade, on Louis VII

of the difficulties of travel and the holy purpose of the enterprise.

Despite the grumbling, women were welcome participants in the crusade. In the First Crusade, many women had accompanied their men and shared their hardships. Eleanor's own reasons for wanting to go have been variously surmised as boredom with palace life in Paris, a love of adventure, and a desire to be at the center of important happenings. As far as religion was concerned, contemporary historians give the impression that, as Meade says, Eleanor "was most religious when her interests and God's interests happened to coincide."

For the vast majority in the 12th century, however, God's interests were of primary importance. Most people in the Europe of the Middle Ages were generally given to thoughts of saving their souls and preparing themselves for heaven. To medieval Christians, seeing the Holy Land and praying at its shrines was one of the greatest, if not *the* greatest, experiences life had to offer. For many the attraction was indeed deeply religious; for others it was an escape from poverty or the law or unhappy personal situations; for still others it was a passport to travel, adventure, and the unknown.

The Second Crusade, originally intended to start out in the spring of 1147, was delayed while elaborate and complicated preparations were made. Taxes were raised all over Europe under pressure from Pope Eugenius to pay for this enormous and costly enterprise. Decisions had to be made as to whether the crusading armies should go the long way by land as in the First Crusade, or travel the shorter and possibly safer, but more expensive, sea routes. Finally, it was decided to go the cheaper way — by land.

Permission for the French Crusaders to march safely through areas of Germany, Hungary, and Greece had to be obtained and guides hired to help the thousands of Crusaders through these foreign lands. Issues such as supplies and the best way to avoid creating undue disturbances among local populations had to be considered. Finally, the Crusaders assembled a caravan carrying tents, food

THE METROPOLITAN MUSEUM OF ART, GIFT OF GEORGE D. PRATT, 1930

A stained glass depiction of the devil, typical of European medieval craftsmanship. The Crusaders brought with them to the Holy Land a religious intolerance not generally found under the ruling Muslims, who, for the most part, left the local Jewish and Christian populations in peace.

supplies, and weapons, that stretched for miles behind the throngs of eager men and women headed toward Jerusalem.

On June 11, 1147, the pope himself, who had crossed the Alps in order to come to the crusade's starting point at Saint Denis, Abbé Suger's abbey, just outside Paris, blessed King Louis and his armies and gave God's approval to this "holy war." Joy and excitement filled the air, and this mood continued all that summer as the Crusaders made their way — often doing as much as ten or twenty miles a day — through France and central Europe. They were frequently joined by enthusiastic crowds in the various French provinces and by thousands of people in Germany alone. The seemingly fortunate Second Crusade, confident of its right and might under the banners of Christendom (the Christian world), had begun.

Eleanor of Aquitaine, the 25-year-old queen of France, full of high spirits as she rode sideways on the "chair saddle" strapped to her horse, was in the forefront of the optimistic travelers going to Jerusalem on "God's business." The general feeling was that only blessings, to say nothing of victory, lay ahead for the Crusaders.

In these early days of the crusade a strict routine was followed in the camps from the nobility on down. Each dawn, preparations were made for that day's march, tents were taken down, and cooking fires were extinguished; in the late afternoon, while a new camp was set up by their servants, the nobles and ladies in Eleanor's area bathed, changed, and then ate near the campfires. Minstrels sang, storytellers entertained, and laughter and lightheartedness prevailed. The Aquitainians were the most merry and the least religious-minded crusaders. Apparently some of the others, Louis's people especially, disapproved of this holiday-like behavior on such a holy mission. It continued to be whispered that the queen was more concerned with worldly than spiritual affairs, despite the Masses she attended and the part she took in daily prayers.

In September 1147 the expedition reached Constantinople, the ancient capital of the Eastern Ro-

King Louis VII takes the crusading vow before Bernard for the Second Crusade. Religious fervor was not the only reason European Christians journeyed to the Holy Land — opportunities for trading and for winning land holdings also induced nobles and commoners alike to join the cause.

The abbey at Saint Denis, where Bernard blessed Louis VII and the Crusaders. Wrote Abbé Suger, who oversaw the church's construction in the new, Gothic style: "It is only through symbols of beauty that our poor spirits can raise themselves from things temporal to things eternal." Eleanor and the king had attended Saint Denis's dedication in 1144.

man (or Byzantine) Empire. This city on the Bosporus, a narrow strait of water dividing a portion of the continents of Europe and Asia, had been named in honor of the Roman Emperor Constantine. He had converted from paganism (a belief in many gods) to Christianity a thousand years before, establishing Christianity as the state religion of the declining Roman Empire. Constantinople is now called Istanbul and is the largest city in Turkey, but in Eleanor's time it was the enormously wealthy stronghold of the Christian Emperor Manuel Comnenus, who governed the Eastern Roman Empire.

The French Crusaders were awed by the glistening domes of the spectacular city. Louis and Eleanor, together with their most noble lords and ladies, were treated royally by the Greek emperor. There were Masses, feasts, and elaborate entertainments provided in honor of the French rulers. The grandeur of the palaces and buildings, the luxury and beauty of the parks, fountains, paintings, and statues all made the visitors marvel. In Europe, there was nothing like it.

Eleanor, who had been brought up in sophisticated surroundings, had never dreamed of such splendor. In fact the Greek empress, Irene, and her ladies considered the French queen very provincial. They thought her unfeminine as well for wanting to make the difficult journey to Jerusalem. Historian Meade states that the two weeks the French spent in Constantinople, in October 1147, were the real beginning of Eleanor's bid for freedom from her husband. Here she had an opportunity to compare his monk-like simplicity with the polish and wealth of the emperor. Eleanor put great value on wealth and power; her already low opinion of Louis now sank even lower.

With regret, the Crusaders led their hordes of followers away from the glories of Constantinople in the golden October weather, and continued on their way to save Jerusalem. However, Louis delayed outside the imperial capital to wait for more troops to arrive. Not only was precious time lost by this error in judgment, but most of the food supplies stored up for the journey to Antioch, their first destination

> *Raymond of Antioch was such a man as the queen could recognize proudly as one of her race and blood. He was, like the other members of her ducal house, tall, handsome, and well knit; in war brave as a lion; in feats of skill and endurance unsurpassed.*
> —RICHARD BARBER
> British historian

in the Middle East, were used up almost at once. Still, they made good progress for the next few months. They continued to buy supplies, at great expense, from whatever towns they happened to pass through. By late January 1148, the Crusaders were high in the southern mountains of Asia Minor (present-day Turkey). It being the rainy season, the Crusaders had chosen the mountain trek to avoid the flooded river valleys.

Then the Crusaders, nobles and commoners alike, began to experience real misery. They suffered from freezing weather and constant rain, which made for great difficulties with the horses and clumsy wagon trains. After their supplies ran out there was nowhere to buy food and general starvation seemed the immediate enemy. They did not know at this point that the German part of the crusading army, which had gone ahead, had been destroyed by the Turks and had all its supplies and gold taken; nor did they know that the Turks were now in hiding, waiting to ambush them. When the time was just right the Turks mounted a surprise attack on the vulnerable Crusaders. Familiar with this mountainous region, the Turks charged on small, tough ponies, yelling wildly, and showered the Crusaders with arrows. For the Europeans, it was a complete disaster. In the ensuing battle, there was a terrific amount of bloodshed and loss of life.

Although both Louis and Eleanor escaped unharmed, the queen's already shaky reputation with the Crusaders worsened, for it was one of her Aquitainian vassal lords who had led the Crusaders into the exact area where the Turks were lying in wait. The chronicles make it clear that this tragedy — so far away from the crusade's destination and with such awful waste of life and property — was blamed on Eleanor, or at least on her influence. Those who survived, including the king and queen, struggled toward the coast and, as soon as possible, boarded ships bound for the old Syrian city of Antioch. Seven thousand foot soldiers had to be left behind because there were not enough ships for everyone. It was learned much later that those who had been left, in the hope that they would somehow find a way to get to the Holy Land, had quickly converted to Islam, the Muslim faith, after being forced to choose between conversion and death.

After three exhausting weeks at sea, Louis and Eleanor led an exhausted and bedraggled company to the shores of Antioch sometime in March 1148. Eleanor's uncle, Prince Raymond of Antioch, who was the youngest brother of Duke William X of Aquitaine, welcomed them all, especially his niece, with open arms.

Raymond had come to Syria more than 10 years earlier, and had become its ruler by taking the child-princess Constance as his bride. He and his niece had a great deal in common. They each had quick

Knights of the Fourth Crusade storm into Constantinople, or Byzantium, in 1204, settling a long dispute between the western kingdoms and the Eastern Roman Empire. When the armies of the Second Crusade arrived on the banks of the Bosporus, in 1147, this eastern capital of Christendom was the most spectacularly wealthy and beautiful city in all of Europe. Eleanor was awestruck by Constantinople's splendor.

The Crusaders in action en route to Jerusalem. When a surprise attack by the Muslim Turks decimated the French forces, the survivors made their way to Antioch, a crusader state ruled by Eleanor's uncle, Prince Raymond. There, relations between Louis and Eleanor — aggravated by differences over how the expedition should continue — deteriorated still further.

minds, a love of luxury, and strong practical natures. Raymond was sympathetic to Eleanor's wish to be free of her husband. Raymond also convinced his niece of the advisability of his plan to have the French army recapture Edessa, which the Turks had taken four years before. In this way, Raymond argued, the future safety of Jerusalem, as well as that of his own city of Antioch, would be assured.

The comforts of the palace, and the general admiration she received at her uncle's court quickly restored Eleanor's health and spirits. Louis, in spite of his leadership in the crusade and his deep concern for the safety of the holy shrines, played a lesser role in Antioch than his wife. We are told by the chroniclers that although she was already pushing for a separation, he "continued to cherish her with an unreasoning love."

Antioch, an ancient city, pagan in its origins and now under Christian control, had much of its past atmosphere and art intact. Louis was deeply disappointed to find so many non-Christian interests and shrines in an area bordering the Holy Land. Eleanor, on the other hand, who in her childhood had seen Muslim traders and Moors, or Arabs from Spain, in her native land, felt at home in this colorful, exotic world.

Louis was shocked that Christians and Muslims not only lived peacefully side by side in Antioch, but that there had even been interfaith marriages. He felt that his mission in going on the crusade had been betrayed. He had not made such sacrifices on the voyage to the Holy Land in order to aid Raymond's private interests. Before deciding on any battle plan — and certainly not the one Raymond was proposing — he was determined to pray at the holy places in the city of Jerusalem. Eleanor, however, was unwilling to leave the delights and companionship she had found in Antioch — or, indeed, to go anywhere with Louis. But her husband was so jealous and anxious to be with her that he actually seized her by force from her uncle's palace, and took her, as he would an angry prisoner, to Jerusalem. This occurrence, together with Louis's refusal to help Raymond's military plans, put an unpleasant end to whatever relationship there had been between the two men — a rift that was to have disastrous consequences.

The city of Jerusalem, nestled in its hills, the sun making its domes and stone walls gleam like gold, is an impressive sight. For the Crusaders, it was a miracle to behold. Meade explains, "When [they] caught their first glimpse of Jerusalem's white walls, they prostrated themselves on the ground weeping like children and asking forgiveness for their sins . . . they kept vigil together throughout the long night." The Christian rulers of the city led the population in almost prayerful greeting to meet the French forces.

Meanwhile, matters continued to grow more and more tense between Eleanor and Louis. In answer to a letter written by Louis, Abbé Suger, left to ad-

GIRAUDON/ART RESOURCE

An 11th-century French medallion showing the head of Jesus. When the "soldiers of Christ," as the Crusaders were called, finally reached Jerusalem in 1148, they were greeted triumphantly by the local Christians, who had long awaited help.

This 11th-century mosaic portrays Christ's entry into Jerusalem on Palm Sunday. This work is typical of the religious iconography seen by Eleanor and Louis in Byzantium and Jerusalem during the Second Crusade.

minister the kingdom in Louis's absence, suggested that the king stop fretting about his wife until his return to France — the crusade was not to be hindered by Louis's personal problems.

No battles had been fought that would justify the expense and losses of this crusade, and the need for showing Europe some results was strong. To this end the French lords of the area persuaded Louis to mount an attack on the Muslim city of Damascus — the capital of Syria. The lords knew that Louis needed a Christian victory in order for the crusade to appear successful in the eyes of the world, and they saw this as an excuse to seize the fertile land and wealth of Damascus, the only Muslim ally of the Christian states. In July 1148, after successfully storming the city's protecting walls, Louis unwisely instructed his army to camp in an area without food or water. When the defenders of Damascus rained arrows on the attackers, killing and wounding hundreds, Louis ordered a retreat. Some said that treachery was involved, that Raymond, together with other Frankish barons, had taken bribes from the leader of Damascus out of spite toward Louis. Others thought it was Louis's lack of political understanding and poor leadership skills that had lost the battle for the Crusaders. Whatever the reason, the French king had no victory to bring home. Rather he had piled still more failures and deaths upon his already heavily burdened conscience.

Frustrated in military matters and miserable about his faltering marriage, Louis was in a sad state. For about a year he delayed going back to France, staying in Jerusalem with his bitter wife and the remainder of his army, praying and doing penance for his sins. Neither letters from Abbé Suger, nor the righteous indignation of his people at home, nor even the queen's negative attitude, moved him. Perhaps he felt safest on all sides by staying right where he was. Eleanor spent this time sightseeing in Jerusalem. But, by now, as Meade says, Eleanor was bored with the city's narrow, winding streets, "the stalls of the Armenian merchants in the bazaars, . . . the Muslim scribes and

THE NEW YORK PUBLIC LIBRARY PICTURE COLLECTION

These Byzantine earrings made of gold, pearls, and precious stones date from the 11th and 12th centuries. Eleanor was greatly impressed by the opulence of many cities in the Eastern Roman Empire and Latin Kingdoms, which lay at the center of the major east-west trade routes for such luxury items as silks, perfumes, and exotic spices.

the Jews and the black slaves, and . . . the swaying camel caravans bearing sacks of Indian spices . . . from Tibet."

Louis keenly felt the failure of his holy mission and it was not until April 1149 that the couple and their followers finally left the Middle East. They

A jeweled ivory hand from 12th-century France with a title engraved on it, "hand of justice of the kings of France." The formation of the fingers is a recurring religious symbol associated with Christ.

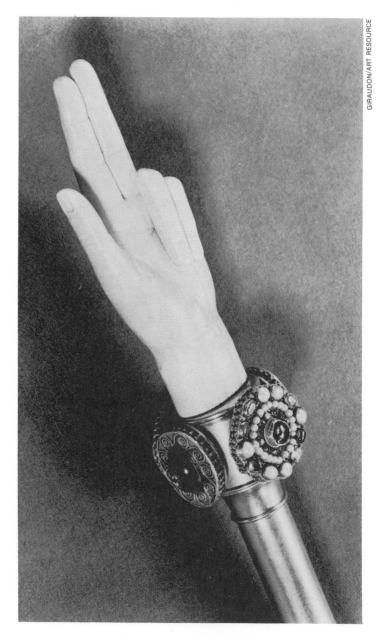

crossed the Aegean and the Mediterranean seas, the king in one ship, the queen and her ladies in another. Storms and misadventures separated the ships and it was a few months before they landed, separately but safely, on the southern coast of Italy. In Sicily, the large island off Italy's southwest coast, Eleanor learned of the recent death of her uncle and friend, Raymond of Antioch. Turkish forces had attacked his city (perhaps inspired by Louis's defeat at Damascus the summer before), and Raymond's troops were beaten. Raymond himself was beheaded in the battle. Rightly or wrongly, Eleanor blamed Louis for creating the circumstances that led to the awful death of the young and splendid Raymond of Antioch, and some historians believe this tragedy broke the last string tying Eleanor to some sense of duty toward her husband.

A miniature painting from the 13th century depicts crusading knights crossing the Mediterranean Sea. Wrote William of Tyre of the failed Second Crusade "It remains a mystery . . . why our Lord should suffer the French, who of all the people in the world . . . most honor Him, to be destroyed by the enemies of religion."

49

4

Changes

The royal couple returned to Paris, where they received a cool reception. The failure of the Second Crusade and the terrible loss of life and waste of vast resources that it entailed, Louis's inability to protect the Christian shrines and palaces in the Holy Land from desecration, and the queen's difficult behavior had all taken a toll on the pair's popularity. Nobles who had returned from the crusade earlier had brought home news of its disasters and misadventures, from the massacre in the mountains to the disgrace at Damascus. Religious leaders believed that the crusade had failed because God had been displeased with the Europeans; others, looking for more practical reasons, blamed Louis's lack of leadership and timidity in decision-making. Eleanor received a large share of the blame for what was seen as her negative influence on and her scornful attitude toward Louis. Much bitter gossip was spread about the way she had spent time luxuriating at her Uncle Raymond's palace in Antioch, and few good words were said for the queen who had not been capable of producing a son and heir to the French throne.

It is of the nature of terrestrial things to change and perish. Prosperity should not swell the heart of man, nor misfortune overwhelm his courage.
POPE EUGENIUS
on the failure of the
Second Crusade

Eleanor and Henry Plantagenet, 12th-century stone carving originally from the Church of Nôtre Dame du Bourg, Langon. A number of such sculptures were made to commemorate the couple's 1152 "progress," or tour, through Eleanor's lands. The goal of the progress was twofold: to acquaint the Aquitainians, always distrustful of outsiders, with Henry; and to erase from Eleanor's realm the influence and memory of Louis VII.

Plaque on the tomb of Geoffrey Plantagenet, count of Anjou and father of Henry II. Through his mother Matilda's link to William the Conquerer, the Norman duke who had subdued England in 1066, Henry II claimed the English throne as his own in 1154.

The storm-tossed journey home had caused Eleanor to show signs of severe strain, both physical and emotional. It has been suggested that the experiences and hardships of the crusade, coupled with the news of her uncle's sudden and terrible death, had caused her to suffer a kind of breakdown. Still, she and Louis had stopped in Tusculum, Italy, on their way home, to see the pope, who had taken up temporary residence in this small town a few miles from Rome. Desperately, she pleaded with Pope Eugenius to grant her an annulment of her marriage to Louis, but was refused.

Although he did not want to be parted from Eleanor, Louis himself, always concerned about the state of his soul, began to doubt the justness of their marriage in the eyes of God. Pope Eugenius had forgotten his disappointment over the failure of the crusade so dear to his heart and warmly welcomed the young couple. He told them to make up their differences and try again. Apparently they attempted to follow the pope's advice, because sometime in 1150 they had a second child, a daughter named Alix. Fate seemed to take a hand in Alix's birth, for if the child had been a boy, Eleanor would never have been allowed her freedom. As it was, in March 1152, after 15 years of marriage, she was finally liberated from her husband. Louis and the pope had been persuaded that Eleanor would never be able to give him the needed male heir, and, at the price of giving up her two daughters, Eleanor reclaimed both her lands and her liberty. Once more she was duchess of Aquitaine.

But only two months later, in May 1152, at Poitiers, Eleanor married a young prince of 18, almost 12 years her junior, who was to become King Henry II of England. Although the shock heard throughout Europe, and especially in Paris, was like "a mighty thunderclap," the decision was not quite as sudden as it must have seemed. In the summer of 1151, both Henry, duke of Normandy, and his father, Count Geoffrey V of Anjou, had come to pay homage to their overlord, King Louis. Geoffrey and Eleanor would certainly have been acquainted, since the province of Anjou was near her childhood home. She would certainly have heard of the fierce and dashing count who had served in military campaigns with her father. Known as Geoffrey the Fair because of his striking handsomeness, the count of

Anjou was also called Geoffrey Plantagenet, *plantagenet* being the Old French word for a shrub that grows yellow flowers, a sprig of which he always wore in his hat or helmet. (The nickname stuck and became the family name of all the English kings for the next 300 years, from Henry II to Henry VI.)

Henry, duke of Normandy, was much more than simply the heir of the count of Anjou. His mother, Matilda, was the widow of the German Emperor Henry V of the Holy Roman Empire, encompassing Germany, Austria, and parts of Italy; and the granddaughter of William the Conqueror, the duke of Normandy who had conquered England from the Saxons and become its king in 1066. A shrewd, intelligent, cultivated woman, forceful in her own right, Matilda's second marriage, to Geoffrey, 15 years her junior, was a political move made to insure the succession of kingships and bases of power in Europe. Henry Fitz-Empress, or son of the empress, as the young duke of Normandy was called, was being groomed to become a king, and king of England at that. Shrewd, energetic, and self-confident, he was the very opposite of the monkish Louis. Eleanor supposedly fell madly in love with him. Considering that she had just been released from a husband she did not care for, that she was a woman of strong feelings, determination, and imagination, and that she was now 30 years old and in the prime of her life, her strong attraction to this compelling, virile young man is believable. The worldly and politically astute Eleanor of Aquitaine understood that Henry would have a brilliant future, and saw that through Henry, she might once again become a queen. Apparently the attraction was mutual, not only on the very strong grounds of the additional power, territories, and wealth such a marriage would bring. The duchess of Aquitaine's great beauty and charm made the alliance desirable from a romantic as well as a political standpoint.

For Eleanor, whose circumstances made her less independent than she would have liked to be, there were still further reasons for the marriage. In 1152, 30-year-old women were not considered young, and a certain stigma was attached to unmarried women

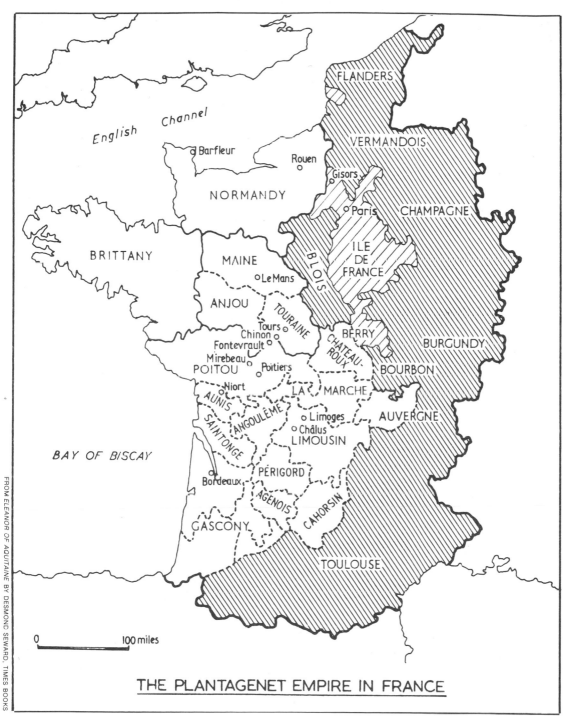

THE PLANTAGENET EMPIRE IN FRANCE

The Plantagenet empire in France. With marriages in the Middle Ages having both love and politics as motivating factors, it is not surprising that Louis, upon learning of Eleanor's marriage to Henry II, sought to counter the loss of Poitou and Aquitaine provinces by sending an army against Henry's Normandy holdings.

An illustration of "hawking," a popular pastime of the nobles in Norman England. Eleanor, used to the comforts of Aquitaine, was unprepared for the harsher conditions and political anarchy she found upon coming to the island in 1154.

of that age. Also she was aware that a woman alone in her position was especially vulnerable to those who envied her wealth and power. For example, there had been an unsuccessful attempt to kidnap her right after her release from her marriage. Nevertheless it was a strong combination of love and ambition that made her give up her liberty and her duchy of Aquitaine. "Her need for independence," says Meade, "converged with an overwhelming passion to rule." Eleanor felt that linking her destiny to Henry's made good practical as well as romantic sense.

Louis's immediate response to the shock of Eleanor and Henry's marriage — as well as the loss of the riches of Aquitaine and Poitou as his daughters' rightful inheritance — was to launch an attack against Henry's province of Normandy. This turned out to be another of Louis's military blunders. Henry's swift counterattack destroyed whatever obstacles were in his path, especially in the Vexin, a disputed territory between Normandy and Île de France (the capital province of the king) and in Touraine, another rich and powerful province. After his victory, Henry joined Eleanor in Poitiers and accompanied her on a royal progress such as she had often made with her father. Although her vassals and subjects loved their duchess, they had resented Louis and now were mistrustful of Henry.

Still, the newlyweds seemed happy, and were received throughout their provinces with laughter and song. Crowds of nobles and ladies, poets, and minstrels accompanied them everywhere. Enormous feasts were given in great halls blazing with hundreds of candles. There were lavish entertainments, songs of love and war were sung, and Eleanor often added tales of her own adventures in Constantinople, Antioch, and Jerusalem. The energetic young Henry particularly enjoyed hunting and falconry.

When Henry was in a good mood, all was well; when he got annoyed, however, he would throw a temper tantrum. The "Angevin temper," as the temper of those from Anjou was called, was reputedly vicious. (Count Geoffrey V, Henry's father, who had

died a few months before his son's marriage to Eleanor, was said to scream and almost foam at the mouth when angered.) During these episodes of insanity those around him — the queen, his followers, and advisers — would just stand by and let these fits run their course. At that time it was rumored that the Angevins were born of the devil. When he first saw Henry as a small child, Bernard of Clairvaux made a statement that was later often repeated: "From the devil he came, to the devil he will go."

The royal tour had been undertaken to acquaint Henry with Eleanor's subjects, lands, and re-

The coronation of King Fulk of Jerusalem, Henry II's grandfather. It was Fulk's death that emboldened the Muslims to attack Edessa in 1144, which in turn had prompted the pope's call for the Second Crusade.

Part of the famous Bayeux tapestry, possibly stitched by Henry II's mother, the Empress Matilda, and her ladies, chronicling the 1066 Norman defeat of England by William the Conquerer. The Latin inscription tells the story of this historic event.

sources. But soon he went away, gathering men and ships for his coming campaign against England. Eleanor, now duchess of Normandy in addition to her other titles, made her new headquarters in one of her husband's main cities, Angers. To her castle flocked poets and artists, the best of the new generation. Coming from Poitou and other provinces, their fortunes would rise along with the rising stars of Eleanor and Henry. In Angers, Eleanor created a court devoted to the arts and worldly pleasures, much as had existed in the time of Duke William IX. A new literature emerged from this atmosphere, a poetic, chivalric literature recounting tales of knights and their ladies, of brave deeds and romantic quests.

But these days of romantic indulgence were soon over, and in 1154 Eleanor joined her husband and mother-in-law, Matilda, in the city of Rouen, the capital of Normandy. Henry had recently returned there after a triumphant campaign in England, where he had gone to battle for his right to succeed to the English throne. As it turned out, the current ruler, King Stephen, promised it to him without bloodshed since his son and heir, Prince Eustace, had died from food poisoning the previous summer in 1153. Not yet 20 years old, Henry had everything

Had she ever been inclined to think of him as a raw, inexperienced youth whom she could dominate and advise, she would have realized she made a mistake during this period.
—MARION MEADE historian, on the early years of Eleanor and Henry II's marriage

going for him — his luck was unbroken, his energy boundless, and a son, William, had been born to Henry and Eleanor on the very day that Prince Eustace died.

In October 1154 King Stephen died as suddenly as had his son, and on a cold, foggy December day, after a stormy crossing of the English Channel between France and England, they landed on the English coast — Henry, a pregnant Eleanor, and the baby prince, William, together with their followers. They immediately pressed on to London where they were joyfully welcomed by the populace. Preparations were hastily made for the coronation of the royal pair, and on the Sunday before Christmas 1154, Henry and Eleanor were proclaimed king and queen of England in Westminster Abbey.

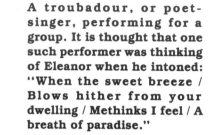

A troubadour, or poet-singer, performing for a group. It is thought that one such performer was thinking of Eleanor when he intoned: "When the sweet breeze / Blows hither from your dwelling / Methinks I feel / A breath of paradise."

A 13th-century tapestry shows court musicians. Such scenes characterized the early days of Eleanor's marriage to Henry II, when she was able to indulge in her favorite pursuit. Eleanor became the patroness of some of the most talented troubadours in Europe, inspiring adoration in verse.

5

Queen of England

Eleanor's first impressions of her new kingdom were mixed. While the enthusiasm of the crowds that had greeted her on her arrival and at her coronation pleased her, 12th-century London itself was another story. Eleanor missed the familiar landscape of her native land and the culture in which she felt most at home. But since her passion was to rule, Eleanor set out to discover her new country, going on long progresses with her tireless husband. Since she had produced two heirs (having given birth to a second son, in February 1155, christened Henry after his father), and transferred her wealth and lands to the English crown, the English looked upon Eleanor as a prize.

Eleanor's firstborn, Prince William, died at the age of three in 1156, leaving the infant Prince Henry the heir to the English throne. In rapid succession, Eleanor gave birth to six more children: Princess Matilda was born in June 1156, the prince who would become the legendary Richard the Lion-Hearted arrived in September 1157, and another prince, Geoffrey, appeared on the scene in 1158. Two more daughters were soon added — Princess Eleanor in September 1161, and Princess Joanna

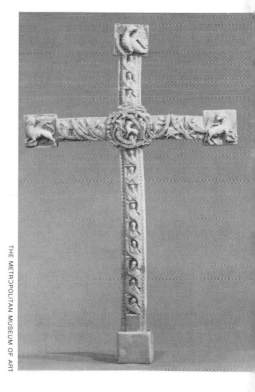

THE METROPOLITAN MUSEUM OF ART

Thomas Becket, controversial churchman and royal adviser, engages in a dispute with King Henry II. Becket lived a life of luxury as chancellor of England, but he became much more ascetic when named archbishop of Canterbury, and subsequently came to oppose the king on many important issues.

This 12th-century English ivory cross with carvings shows the lamb of God and other symbols of Christian evangelists.

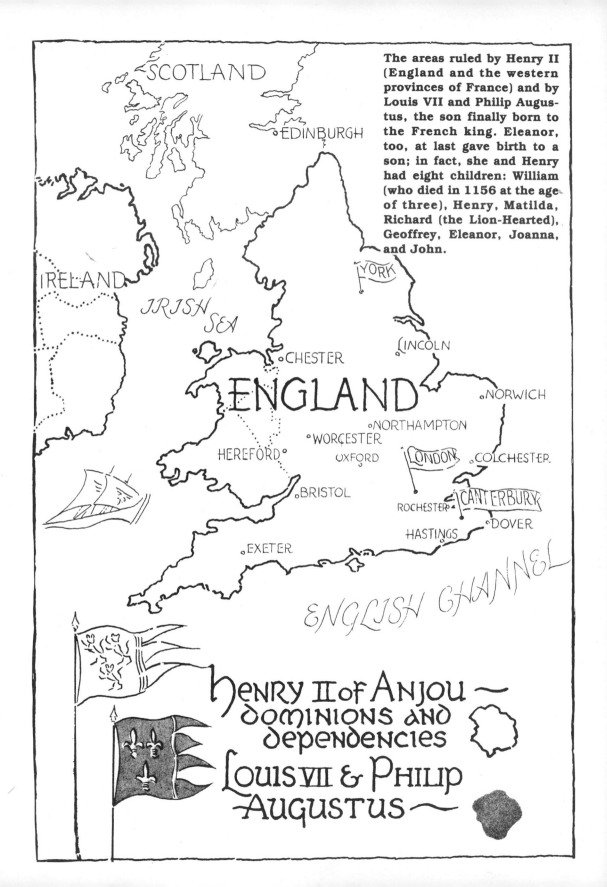

The areas ruled by Henry II (England and the western provinces of France) and by Louis VII and Philip Augustus, the son finally born to the French king. Eleanor, too, at last gave birth to a son; in fact, she and Henry had eight children: William (who died in 1156 at the age of three), Henry, Matilda, Richard (the Lion-Hearted), Geoffrey, Eleanor, Joanna, and John.

SCOTLAND

EDINBURGH

IRELAND

IRISH SEA

YORK

LINCOLN

CHESTER

ENGLAND

NORWICH

NORTHAMPTON

WORCESTER

HEREFORD

OXFORD

LONDON

COLCHESTER

BRISTOL

ROCHESTER

CANTERBURY

HASTINGS

DOVER

EXETER

ENGLISH CHANNEL

HENRY II of ANjOU ~
dOMINIONS ANd
dEPENDENCIES
LOUIS VII & PHILIP
AUGUSTUS ~

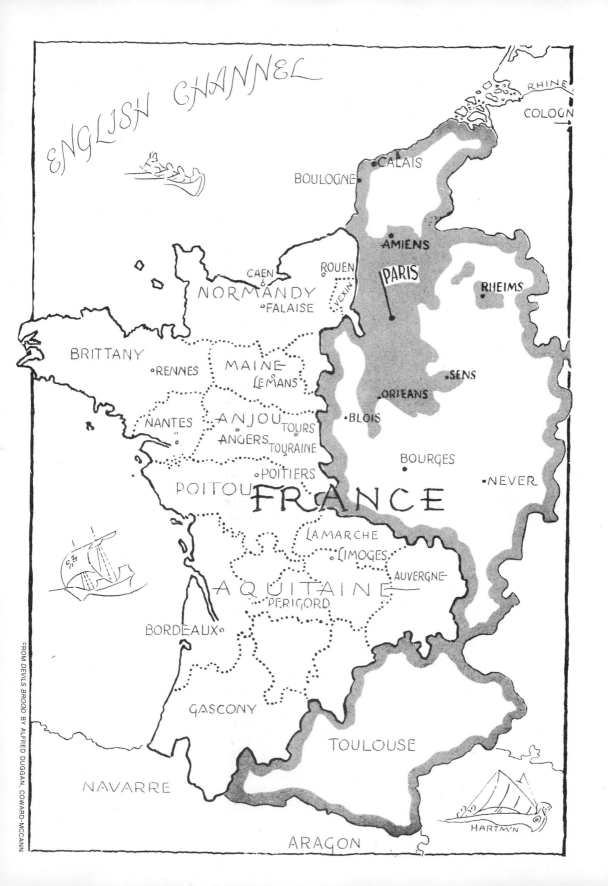

ENGLISH CHANNEL

RHINE
COLOGN

CALAIS
BOULOGNE

AMIENS
PARIS

RHEIMS

CAEN
ROUEN
NORMANDY
VEXIN
FALAISE

BRITTANY

RENNES
MAINE
LE MANS

SENS

ORLEANS

NANTES
ANJOU
TOURS
ANGERS
TOURAINE

BLOIS

BOURGES

POITIERS

POITOU
FRANCE

NEVER

LA MARCHE
LIMOGES
AUVERGNE

AQUITAINE
PERIGORD

BORDEAUX

GASCONY

TOULOUSE

NAVARRE

HARTM'N

ARAGON

FROM DEVILS BROOD BY ALFRED DUGGAN, COWARD-MCCANN

in October 1165. The last Plantagenet child, Prince John, born in December 1166, was nicknamed "John Lackland" because his parents had no more territories for him to inherit.

Inheritance was very much on King Henry's mind at this period, and much as he was interested in England, his main interests lay in his Norman and Aquitainian possessions. Still, it was he who brought England back from the chaos from which it had suffered under the previous king; it was he who laid the foundation for English Common Law, a code of law that would provide the basis of the modern English and American legal systems. Historian Meade says that "no ruler of England, before or after, would so strongly influence the development of its institutions as Henry Plantagenet, and so thoroughly would he do his work that, after his passing, the royal government would be able to function, if need be, without a king." It was Henry Plantagenet who fused all his diversified and enormous holdings in France, England, and Scotland (later he added Ireland, too), sometimes through negotiation, and sometimes in battle, into one empire. Where did this man get this sense of his own power and his belief in the rightness of his political understandings and actions?

Perhaps the strongest known influence on Henry's outlook was his mother, Matilda, who had spent 20 years grooming him for kingship and intriguing for his claims. Henry valued Matilda's opinions on public matters. No less formidable a character than her son, Matilda Empress (she was previously married to the Holy Roman Emperor), as she was known, was intellectual, reserved, and disciplined. Though a stern parent, she could relax now that her task of getting Henry on the English throne had been accomplished. A patron of culture no less than Eleanor, it was philosophers and men of wisdom who were favored at her court in Rouen, Normandy, rather than the poets and troubadours who basked in the warmth and light of Eleanor's patronage. Some historians think that Matilda was the main source of her son's iron will. Others have suggested that it was Henry's mother who taught him "to avoid

triflers and hangers-on and to closet himself in his
[rare] leisure with men of wisdom and with books,"
as historian Amy Kelly puts it.

The fact that Henry's mother seemed more important to him than his wife was only one of several
grievances Eleanor had against Henry. Though the
royal couple apparently cared for one another, power
struggles were frequent. Henry may have valued
Eleanor's input in state matters, but he was not
about to allow her equality of power, at least not

**Bishop from a set of ivory
chessmen, dating from 12th-
century England. Eleanor
encouraged literary and intellectual pursuits in her
new kingdom, bringing with
her to England the elegance
and sophistication of her
court at Aquitaine.**

Scenes from "Life of St. Thomas," a 13th-century
French manuscript, include "Thomas excommunicat-
ing his enemies and arguing with Henry and Louis."
Becket's friendship with Henry II and swift rise to prom-
inence sparked some jealousy and resentment in Eleanor
and led her to carve out an independent life quite apart
from the king and the circles of state power.

in England. Although she had proved herself a woman of wisdom and experience since their marriage, it was not Eleanor to whom he turned after his mother's death. The king wanted another man to represent him when he was abroad on Angevin business. Kelly tells us he wanted ". . . a man of large ability whom he could trust as [himself], a chancellor and something more, an intimate whose loyalty and intelligence should enlarge his own administration, yet who should, in the last resort, be subject to the royal will." His choice fell on a certain Thomas Becket.

Becket was an Englishman of Norman ancestry who had risen in court circles from what we today would call a middle-class family. He had been groomed for public service by the archbishop of Canterbury himself. (This was the highest church position in England, next in authority to the pope in Rome.) A man of great ability, charm, and integrity, Becket had been a student in Paris under the philosopher Peter Abelard at the time Eleanor had come there as a bride. He had traveled widely on business for the archbishop, and was knowledgeable both in the ways of courts and the high places of the Church. Being 15 years older than Henry, and therefore approximately the same age as Eleanor, Becket was mature enough for the king to listen to and young enough for him to have as a personal friend. They became remarkably close, and the young ruler made Becket his chancellor, or chief minister of state. Becket was to go along on all Henry's travels and assist in conducting the affairs of the kingdom.

Eleanor was not pleased with the closeness and affection that was evident between the two men. A chronicler of the time wrote that the king "bestowed upon [Becket] many revenues . . . and received him so much into his esteem and familiarity that throughout the kingdom, there was none equal, save the king alone." In other words, Henry heaped huge amounts of money as well as palaces, fine clothes, jewels, and furnishings on his new chancellor. Eleanor felt that her husband thought more of Thomas Becket and spent more time with him than he did with her; she felt that the only equal of

The residence of Thomas Becket in Tarring, England. Henry II thought that Becket would be an acquiescent archbishop, one who would assure smooth relations between church and state. But Becket decided that as the highest church official in England, he was answerable only to the pope and God.

the king should be his queen.

Soon all Europe knew of Becket's wealth, splendor, and influence with Henry. Although the queen's jealousy of what she considered her exclusion from power was very much present, she was so occupied in those early years of her marriage that her jealousy did not prevail. She continued to bear children while traveling extensively back and forth between the continental provinces and England. She often joined her husband abroad, and sometimes made solo tours of her new land. She had control of her own monies, "the queen's gold," and occasionally substituted most effectively for the king in his absence as *judiciar*, or judge, both in England and France.

As she had in Anjou and Aquitaine, Eleanor surrounded herself with an elegant and cultured court, where literature, the arts, and manners were raised to heights never before seen in England. The elegance of the household was most important to Eleanor. This elegance was reflected in the candles, gold cups, and fine linens that decorated her fastidiously kept quarters.

The good fortune that had provided Henry with many male heirs had not shone with equal favor on Eleanor's former husband, Louis VII Capet of France, whose second marriage to the Spanish princess Constance, in 1154, had produced only a daughter, Marguerite. Despite the dislike and resentment that Louis and the French still felt toward Eleanor and Henry for having taken Poitou and Aquitaine away from them, they agreed to Henry's plan of betrothing, or promising to marry, the little English Crown Prince Henry to the baby Princess Marguerite Capet. Considering the bad blood between the two families this seems an extraordinary move until we realize that, like all royal marriages, it was contracted to insure successions, cement alliances, and retain lands and power. This marriage was seen as an excellent means of solidifying the future of both the French and English Crowns; what Henry wanted was for *his* future grandson to wear the "double crown" of England and France. But it was a delicate matter and, since the idea was Henry's, it was he who needed to show goodwill. Accordingly, in the summer of 1158, he sent his chancellor, Thomas Becket, to Paris to smooth the way and diplomatically secure the alliance. Becket accomplished this task with so much success that it became clear that this union would, one day, wipe away the memory of the rift between Eleanor and Louis.

The years that followed were full of outbreaks of small wars between many bordering provinces in France, as well as family upheavals that were to have serious political consequences for the futures of Henry and Eleanor. One such event was the unexpected death of Louis's queen, Constance, while giving birth to a second daughter in 1160 and his remarriage a month later to Countess Adèle of Champagne. Not only was the countess one of the richest heiresses in Europe, but in 1165 she was to bear the prince so long awaited by the French. The birth of Philip II, better known as Philip Augustus, threatened Henry's scheme of eventually uniting England and France through marriage. Not one to sit by when any action could be taken, the English king immediately went to war with the French queen's family, making the French understand he would be a force to be reckoned with militarily.

Meanwhile, Thomas Becket's fortunes continued

> To Eleanor's great chagrin, the court over which she should have presided and which no woman in Europe knew better how to conduct, had somehow slipped through her fingers and drifted down the Thames to Thomas Becket's splendid mansion.
> —MARION MEADE
> historian

"Monks at work," from an early 12th-century French manuscript. Henry II grew furious at Becket's public criticism of his rule, and the two gradually became bitter antagonists. Among the matters they differed over were the king's attempts to tax church lands and to try clergymen in the civil courts.

to rise. Not only did he have the responsibility of the education of young Prince Henry, heir to the throne, but he was soon to move from the highest political position in the kingdom to the most important religious one. In 1161 his old patron, the archbishop of Canterbury, died, and Henry decided that Becket would become the new archbishop. Becket was thought by many, including Eleanor, to lack the proper qualifications for the job. First of all, he was neither a priest nor a monk; moreover, he was known to be the "king's man." But Henry stood firm. In Becket he would have an archbishop whose opinions would parallel his own so that church and state would not clash as often as they had in the past. He and Thomas would be of one mind, or so Henry thought.

One of the king's reasons for choosing Becket was that he had decided to have Prince Henry crowned king immediately, thus insuring the succession. Since only the archbishop of Canterbury had the power to perform that ceremony, Henry had no doubt that Becket would be glad to oblige, which he did. For future matters, however, the chronicles make it evident that it was clear to Becket that in accepting this position, ". . . he would lose either the favor of God or that of the king." Eleanor, who had always thought Becket overly ambitious and had resented him for years, proved to be right when she told Henry that she did not think the new archbishop would be satisfied merely to follow the king's wishes.

The changes began immediately upon Thomas's acceptance. He was ordained as a priest in June 1162, and then, within days, became archbishop of Canterbury. Suddenly Becket lost interest in power and worldly things, becoming dedicated to "the honor of God" instead. He stopped living in the luxury to which he had lately become accustomed, and adopted the austere life of a religious monk. To Henry's dismay, Becket also returned the Great Seal of England, the symbol of the chancellor's power. Becket intended this gesture to serve as a warning that he was going to follow his own conscience, not Henry's. According to one of his contemporaries, the new archbishop was fast becoming "a bright candle on God's candlestick." Though tensions between Becket and Henry continued to mount, the old affection and closeness survived for a while. Soon, however, events put archbishop and king in opposite corners. The first serious rumbles were heard in the summer of 1163 when Becket criticized the king for collecting a tax, one that had nothing to do with church matters. Henry, furious over Becket's meddling behavior, soon brought matters to a head.

Crime was rampant in England during this period, and the situation was complicated by the fact that church officals were committing many of these crimes, knowing that they were only subject to the Church's jurisdiction and could not be tried in the civil courts under the "king's justice." The king asked the archbishop to turn such criminals over to him, and Becket refused. No matter how much Henry ranted and raved, Thomas would politely answer that he would serve the king faithfully in all matters concerning the king, but that he would do nothing when it was a matter of "the honor of God." Their friendship and trust quickly became a bitter personal feud that would go on for years.

A 12th-century reliquary, or container for sacred relics. Becket refused to allow Henry's civil courts to acquire jurisdiction over church matters.

6

Poetry, Prison, Politics

Aquitaine had always been a place of refuge for Eleanor. Soon after the birth of her last child, John, Eleanor returned home in 1168. After Henry publicly displayed his love for another woman, the beautiful Rosamond Clifford, Eleanor left him. She proceeded to take her revenge on him and his dream of an expanding empire, a dream in which she had never been granted a role large enough to satisfy her. Everything Eleanor owned went with her. It took seven ships to carry all her goods away. Her people were glad to have a revival of the ducal court and to be out from under the oppression to which their duchess's two husbands had subjected them, while Eleanor used the power of her own domain to recover both her wealth and freedom. Such behavior was so extraordinary for a woman, even if she was Eleanor of Aquitaine, that people in Paris and London talked of nothing else. Henry, seemingly agreeable to this unofficial separation, probably calculated that Eleanor's presence there would calm the rebellious Aquitainians. As a way of protecting his interests, he escorted her to Poitiers and had his heir, Henry, declared future overlord of his brother Richard, Eleanor's favorite and her chosen heir of Poitou and Aquitaine.

A sculpture of Minerva, the Roman goddess of wisdom. According to biographer Amy Kelly, Eleanor, determined not to play a secondary role, dedicated her new regime at Poitiers "neither to Mars nor to the Pope, nor to any king, but to Minerva, Venus (the goddess of love and beauty), and the Virgin."

Illustration from a 15th-century *Romance of the Rose* manuscript; the scene is entitled "The Garden of Love." Increasingly estranged from Henry II, Eleanor returned to her native Aquitaine in 1168 and together with her daughter Marie, countess of Champagne, established in Poitiers a private "court of love," whose basic precept was that women were superior to men.

Once the queen had established her residence in Poitou and had Richard installed, she worked to establish a domain. Eleanor made many royal tours to bring peace to the province and to show off her intended heir, the handsome Richard. They traveled from the Loire River to the Pyrenees mountains, stopping in cities such as Limoges, Bayonne, and Bordeaux. Eleanor, accustomed to being a queen, was now a ruler in her own right. Under her experienced leadership, Poitiers once more became the center of civilized living. "From 1169," Meade says, "Eleanor's two-fold resolution stands out clearly: to cut Aquitaine from the Plantagenet empire insofar as this seemed feasible, and to create for herself a realm that would reflect the splendor of the past and prefigure innovations of the future." And so it continued for five years.

Despite the fact that she had left both her royal husbands, during the next few years at Poitiers Eleanor had practically all the royal and high-born

John, youngest son of Eleanor and Henry II, was called "John Lackland" because, by the time he was born, the king had already divided his lands among his older sons. All of Eleanor's children, even those from her marriage to Louis VII, joined her at Poitiers for "education and safekeeping."

youths of the provinces of France, the future rulers and marriage prizes of Europe, in her charge for "education and safekeeping." Her own children were there, including her eldest daughter by Louis — Marie, now countess of Champagne. Louis VII's other daughters were there as well. Historians have speculated that Louis sent Marie to her mother's court in order to keep an eye on her half-sisters, Marguerite and Alais. Marie of Champagne, an extremely intelligent young woman in her mid-twenties, esteemed for her qualities throughout France, evidently lent a kind of respectability to the court of Poitiers in the eyes of the pious French king.

The same intellect, poetic fire, and capacity to rule characterized both Eleanor and Marie. It is easy to imagine Eleanor's delight at finding such a kindred spirit in a daughter who surely had been brought up to disapprove of her mother, if not to hate her. Historians believe that Marie was a born teacher and that the "court of love" that she and Eleanor created expressed a need that both she and Eleanor felt to teach something useful to the young people at Poitiers court. Marie, whose famous troubadour, Chrétien de Troyes, had put the old story of King Arthur, Lancelot, and Guinevere into poetry and song, wisely made the learning process more desirable by giving the "lessons" in the form of poetry and art. Later in life, according to Kelly, Marie's half-brother and most prominent pupil, Richard the Lion-Hearted, would always speak of Poitiers "as the world's citadel of valor, the seat of courtesy, and the fountainhead of poetic inspiration." The court of Poitiers at this time was the model for the code of chivalry that remained the aristocratic ideal for a long time.

The court of love was based on the idea that women were not only equal, but superior, to men. This code was based on the precepts of the courts of law and feudalism (both systems conceived by men), except here women were the overlords to whom men, their humble vassals, were to pay kneeling homage. Marie, with the help of her chaplain, Andreas Cappelanus, made up the code of manners in which the social behavior of her male subjects would be refined as she saw fit. The details of the

> *Eleanor played a passionate part in a passionate age.*
> —CURTIS HOWE WALKER
> American historian

new chivalry are attributed to Marie, but the guiding spirit is Eleanor's. Woman would be the center and focus; man, her inferior, was to please and serve her. Such service and devotion, she reasoned, would be to men's advantage, because their characters would be improved by the ideal of love. Here, woman was "supreme," Meade informs us, "a goddess to be approached with reverence, and . . . man is her property." The code can thus be interpreted as a bid for power rather than for love. Ultimately the standards of Eleanor's court served to soften the rough, warlike aspects that characterized feudal society.

While Eleanor cultivated the court of love, King Henry fought, planned, and worked unceasingly to forge his empire. After years of bitter quarrels and upheavals, religious and political, between Thomas Becket and the king, Henry's unbroken good fortune suddenly turned. Four of Henry's knights had heard Henry in a particularly wild rage over Becket (who was not present) at his Christmas court in Normandy. These barons took it upon themselves — they later said they thought it was what the king wanted — to return to England, accuse Becket of betraying the king, and murder him in cold blood near the high altar of Canterbury Cathedral. The highest churchman in England had been killed in his own church, on holy ground.

The decline of Henry's power began with the terrible death of Thomas Becket in December 1170. The English king, whose grief was said to be genuine, was held responsible by all of Europe for the archbishop's violent death. Though he disclaimed any knowledge of or desire for the murder, Henry did penance for the deed by allowing himself to be publicly whipped by the monks of Canterbury Cathedral.

Unfortunately for Henry's political future, Becket's murder did not end the archbishop's influence. Almost immediately after his death, miracles were said to take place in Canterbury. For example, a day or two after the murder, a blind woman claimed her sight was restored after touching what was left of the martyr's blood on the stones. The result of all this was that Thomas Becket was nominated for

> **My lord, while Thomas lives, you will not have peace or quiet, or see good days.**
>
> —an English bishop, warning Henry about Thomas Becket

sainthood in the Catholic church.

Kelly states, "As veneration of Saint Thomas grew, the Angevin lost some of his honor among men." He had lost honor among his sons too, and it rankled him that his wife, having gone against his will, had young Henry, Richard, and Geoffrey (John was still a small child) under her spell at the exciting and independent court in Poitiers. Apparently he had no illusions about the boys' feelings for him.

A chronicler of the time described a fresco, or wall painting, that Henry later commissioned at his palace in Winchester, England. It showed a frightening picture: ". . . a great eagle with spread wings [was shown] set upon by four eaglets. Two of the fledglings, with furious beak and claws, wounded the [wings] of the parent bird; a third dug at his vitals; and a fourth, perched upon his neck, clawed at his

The Church of Saint Jean in Poitiers. Under Eleanor's rule, Poitiers became the European center for aristocratic chivalry and elegant living, and many noble families sent their children to be educated there.

Manuscript illustration
showing King Arthur of England and the knights of the
round table. The tale of the
legendary king became so
popular that the Plantagenets made him their ances-
tor. Later, Henry, threatened
by widespread belief that the
beloved Arthur would return
and claim his glory, orga-
nized an archeological expedition to "prove" that Arthur had died.

eyes. Asked what this . . . meant, Henry explained
that the great eagle was himself, and the eaglets
were his four sons. 'Thus will they pursue me till I
die, and that least one whom I now cherish with so
much affection [John], will be the most malig-
nant of them all.' " This prophecy in all essentials
came true.

Though the characters of the young Plantagenets
were very different, they all inherited from the Angevin side the terrible temper that was Henry II's.
Of them, as of him, it was said, "From the devil they

came, to the devil they will go." From the Poitevin side they inherited an instability that was thought to be Eleanor's. Her eldest son, Henry, especially — the Young King, as he was now called — took after her in this respect as in some others. Young Henry was extremely graceful, charming, and unpredictable. Unlike his mother, however, he was easily influenced. It was this eldest son whom Henry loved best and on whom he pinned all his hopes and ambitions. On some level, the Young King was a victim of circumstance, pulled in many directions, with divided loyalties at different times — sometimes to Becket who had been his tutor and in whose household he had, in part, grown up; sometimes to his father's court; at other times to his mother's court at Poitiers.

Richard, his mother's favorite, apparently most resembled his father physically. Kelly says he was "a born strategist and warrior. . . . His mind was quick and his interests were more concentrated and persistent than the young king's. . . . He displayed likewise the Angevin suddenness and violence . . . [and was] more ruthless to conquered foes than the king his father. . . ." On the other hand, as Eleanor's son and heir, he was a true son of Poitou and had the reputation of being a good poet and singer himself, as would befit the great-grandson of William the Troubadour. Legend has it that, years later, when Richard himself was king of England and a prisoner held for ransom, a troubadour who had been searching for him heard him singing from a high fortress castle. The king and troubadour made contact and communicated by cleverly improvising to the tune and rhythm of the song without the guards suspecting that Richard was revealing his place of imprisonment to his rescuers. Richard and his older brother Henry were vividly compared in one of the chronicles: "Henry was a shield, but Richard was a hammer."

Geoffrey and John were more similar to each other than to their two older brothers. Both were shorter than the other two and darker in coloring. Geoffrey, who was said to be the cleverest of the four, was very smooth-talking and manipulative, knowing how to make "black seem white with remarkable contrivance. . . . Shameless and crafty . . . he was reckless, bold, decisive, swift as lightning," according to Kelly. John, as he grew older, shared the same shamelessness and craftiness that he would display so much later in his unhappy and unsuccessful reign as king of England.

In addition to the "empty titles" Henry had given his children, they were all "placed in positions of inevitable rivalry [and] made witness to [various] violent feudal conflicts and domestic scenes" over a period of years, as Kelly points out. To some extent this explains their involvement in schemes against their father, encouraged by a spiteful Eleanor. In 1173, when Henry was on campaign in Ireland, waging war to gain some territories to give to "Lackland" John, his youngest son, rumors reached him there of the doings at the brilliant court of Aquitaine. The rumors included not only the details of the "courtly love" assemblies in which the highest knights of the realms took part, but the news that Poitiers had become "a rendezvous for traitors." He heard that the queen was stirring up revolt against him, not only with those nobles of her own provinces who felt he had dealt harshly with them economically, but with his own sons as well. And now, incredibly, those sons were joining forces with his enemy, Louis VII. As was his custom, Henry sprang into action.

His first move was to take the Young King away from Poitiers and his mother's ideas, and to keep him under his own watchful eye. Young Henry managed to escape from his father and ran away to the protection of his father-in-law, the French king. At the French court in Paris, the Young King gave away pieces of his father's kingdom — or, since his coronation, *his* kingdom, as he considered it — to those barons who had helped him flee from Henry. This was the signal for an uprising against his father, and the Young King got Richard and Geoffrey, still living with their mother in Poitiers, to join his cause. By the late spring of 1173, many other powerful nobles had joined the rebellion. Soon, young Henry and his French allies attacked, and the fire spread from the continent to England. By Septem-

Virgin and child, Greek mosaic. Adoration of the Virgin was a crucial part of Eleanor's court of love, where, according to one historian, woman was "supreme, a goddess to be approached with reverence."

ber, however, Henry's forces, initially taking a beating, had recaptured so many castles and so much territory, that the leaders of the revolt against his authority, headed by King Louis himself, asked for a truce. To Henry's dismay, after the truce was reached all three of his sons went back to Paris with Louis, their overlord for their continental lands.

Eleanor had sided with her sons against her husband for a long time now. Through the archbishop of Rouen in Normandy, Henry wrote Eleanor that he was willing to forget the past and receive her again if she would stop inciting their sons against him. When she failed to answer his letter, Henry responded by ordering his army to wreak havoc in her domains. In the early spring of 1174, Henry's men captured the desperate queen as she was fleeing, disguised as a man, perhaps to put herself under the protection of her overlord and former husband, Louis VII, in Paris. Holding her responsible for all his troubles, Henry may have kept her in a fortress, as she disappeared from view for a few months. In May 1174 Henry disbanded the rest of the court of Poitiers, taking all the highborn ladies, as well as Eleanor herself, back to England as captives. The queen was imprisoned in the stronghold of Salisbury Tower.

Queen Eleanor's imprisonment was not a matter of being kept in a cell or a dark place. The chronicles say she was moved about, first to one castle, then another, and although allowed her own servants, was always under watch, ". . . restrained, denied

This 15th-century manuscript, called *The Fates of Illustrious Men*, depicts the goddess Fortune and her revolving wheel, a popular medieval symbol of the changing nature of fate. In Eleanor's court, the queen sat upon a similar raised platform while passing judgment on matters of love or romantic conduct.

her sovereign liberty, her ancestral revenues, the use of her years of prime," says Kelly. Being deprived of her freedom was extremely difficult for Eleanor; in fact she seems to have emerged with a changed outlook on life. It is said that much of the wisdom, self-discipline, and strength that characterized Eleanor's later life, in contrast to the frivolities of her youth, came from these years of enforced solitude. It is true that she was allowed occasional liberties. Once in a while King Henry would ask her attendance, at such occasions as Christmas or Easter courts, to give the impression of family unity. The royal celebrations featured feasting and often jousting, or formal combat between knights, and a display of wealth and generosity meant to reaffirm the power of the Plantagenets. Eleanor, accustomed to being the center of attention, now had to remain in the background. In fact, she spent most of those long years in relative isolation. It is to her great credit that her spirit and her understanding of life can be said to have grown rather than deteriorated during the 15 years she spent under Henry's thumb.

Henry knew that the queen, though a prisoner, remained, in Kelly's words, "the object of intrigue, the inspiration of her . . . sons and of the turbulent fortune seekers who found their profit in war." What was Henry to do with his captive? In a *Lament for Eleanor* that has come down to us from this period, under the authorship of "Richard le Poitevin," we can hear an echo of the feelings of her sympathizers and Henry's dilemma: "You have been snatched from your own lands and carried away to an alien country. Reared with abundance of all delights, you enjoyed a royal liberty. You lived richly on your own inheritance; you took pleasure in the pastimes of your women, in their songs, in the music of lute and drum. And now you grieve, you weep, you are consumed with sorrow. But come back to your own towns, poor prisoner. Where is your court? Where are the young men of your household? Where are your counselors? . . . You cry out and no one heeds you, for the King of the North holds you in captivity. But cry out and cease not to cry; lift your voice like a trumpet and it shall reach the ears of your sons.

> *A very intelligent woman, sprung from a noble race, but unsteady.*
> —GERVASE OF CANTERBURY
> English monk and
> chronicler, on Eleanor

Model of a Carolingian knight. The Carolingians were an earlier Frankish dynasty that held power from 751 to 987; they were succeeded by the Capetian house — the family of Louis VI and Louis VII.

The day will come when they will deliver you, and you shall come again to dwell in your own lands."

King Henry was well aware of Eleanor's popularity and influence. He considered her a danger as well as an impediment. He would not make Louis's mistake by merely divorcing her, leaving her free to lay claims to her lands. Instead Henry would keep her a prisoner once he had divorced her, so that she could never act against him following their separation. Henry decided to have Eleanor held in the abbey of Fontevrault, on the continent in Angevin territory, where many kings and nobles before him had had their wives confined. Eleanor, however, refused to go. Further complications resulted when Henry took his request for a divorce to the pope — his request was denied.

As if Henry's difficulties with Eleanor weren't enough, his problems with his sons had just begun. Disappointed in and distrustful of his older sons, Henry acquired Irish lands for John, who had been too young to take part in the rebellion, and married him to the richest, most powerful heiress in England, the daughter of the earl of Gloucester. Al-

SNARK/ART RESOURCE

The martyrdom of Thomas Becket, as depicted in a Latin-inscribed English psalmbook from around 1200. In December 1170 four of Henry's knights, after hearing the king rage at Becket's excommunication of two important churchmen, fatally stabbed the archbishop on his altar in Canterbury. The crime shocked all of Europe.

though he kept a strict eye on his three older sons, Henry tried to excuse their treachery, citing their youth, their inexperience, and Eleanor's bad influence on them. The king was especially forgiving of young Henry, and even tried to teach him statecraft, but to no avail. The Young King continued to resent his secondary role; despite his title of "king," Henry believed his father had no intention of giving up any power to him. Meanwhile, his brothers Richard and Geoffrey exercised real authority in Aquitaine and Brittany respectively, even under their father's stricter scrutiny. Richard, in fact, had effectively suppressed a rebellion against him in his provinces of Poitou and Aquitaine, impressing his father with his leadership abilities, to the even greater frustration of the Young King. After 1177 young Henry's position became really intolerable when Henry crowned John king of Ireland, which he had just conquered for him.

While the Young King of England fretted, the old order was slowly changing. It was 1180 and not only was the English king's control of lands and events seriously undermined, but every one of the principal actors in the drama was aging: Henry was 47 and Eleanor, now 58, had been a prisoner for six years. That same year Louis VII died at the age of 59.

Louis's young, tough-minded son, Philip Augustus, decided to challenge Henry's authority. Before Philip did so, however, there was a brief period during which Henry, according to Kelly, devoted "his whole insight and energy to replacing the crumbling pillars of the feudal world with a more enduring structure." One of Henry's main achievements as king was to convert the old, "uncentralized society" with its different customs and laws in neighboring provinces into "a well-functioning organism." Using all his considerable talents, to say nothing of the experience at his command, Henry traveled all over his extensive domains making judicial improvements. He systematized taxes and created a new army as well. Being a king who was capable of learning, Henry surrounded himself with clever and knowledgeable advisers from many walks of life. As a result, a great number of people outside the ar-

Henry does public penance at Becket's tomb in 1174.
Though the king's grief was said to be genuine, most of
Europe and much of his own family held him responsible
for the cold-blooded murder.

THOMAS BECKET
ARCHBISHOP · SAINT · MARTYR
DIED HERE
TUESDAY 29TH · DECEMBER
1170

Becket's tomb in Canterbury Cathedral. Following reports of miracles occurring in Canterbury, the tomb became a shrine to which many Christians made pilgrimages. The martyred Becket was canonized in 1173.

istocracy found their way into governing circles. More and more non-aristocrats began to educate their sons for positions never before attainable, paving the way for a large, more prosperous middle class. No English king before his time, and very few after, could rival Henry's achievements in restructuring English society.

Although the French under Philip Augustus soon started harassing Henry's territories again, it was his own sons fighting among each other that most troubled Henry. Richard, by 1182, was so hated by the barons of the south that they insisted another "acceptable leader" be found. Using his jealousy of Richard's power as bait, the barons persuaded the Young King to step in against his brother. At their father's Christmas court that year, held in Caen, Normandy, Henry himself tried to reconcile the two young men, but they remained estranged. During the next summer, the brothers were again at odds, and when their father tried to intervene, he was almost killed, some said through the Young King's treachery. Then, after stealing from the treasuries of rich monasteries, the Young King fell ill of a fever and was near death. (Some said it was God's punishment for the sacrilege done.) On his deathbed, young Henry begged his father's forgiveness and asked that his mother be released from her long captivity. In June 1183, at the age of 28, the Young King died. When Henry heard the news he was devastated, in spite of all the worry and misery his oldest son had brought him. When Eleanor received the news of the death of her son, she claimed that she did not need to be told, that she had seen it in a dream. She had interpreted a dream in which she saw young Henry with a calm face wearing one crown shining on top of another, dimmer one, to mean that her son was now in the kingdom of heaven. Some historians doubt Eleanor's story; they think the dream story was a tactful way to cover information to which she seems to have had access.

The death of the Young King changed the set of circumstances that had begun in 1169 when Eleanor, by designating Richard her heir of Aquitaine and Poitou, had forced Henry to give his other

> *Few women have had less justice done them in history than Eleanor.*
> —BISHOP STUBBS
> historian

91

*Now every grief and woe and
    bitterness,
The sum of tears that this sad
    century's shed,
Seem light against the death of
    the young king,
And prowess mourns, youth
    stands sorrowful;
No man rejoices in these bitter
    days.*

—BERTRAN DE BORN
French soldier and
troubadour, on the death
of Henry the Young King

sons their specific inheritances. Since young Henry died childless, the queen's favorite, Richard, was now heir to the throne of England. When his father wanted to reapportion inheritances, Richard refused to give back his Aquitainian lands. His 62-year-old mother backed him in this, and the king had to relent because of his wife's rights to her own property. Since Geoffrey, who was already count of Brittany, was soon after killed in an accident in 1186, only John stood to gain by any estrangement between Richard and his father.

Once again, in 1184, the Latin Kingdoms in the Holy Land were falling to the "infidels," and once again Christian Europe was asked to come to their aid by means of a crusade. Henry was asked to lead such a venture, but refused. Then, in 1187, news that Jerusalem itself had fallen changed matters drastically. Both Henry and the French king, Philip Augustus, prepared to lead Christian armies to-

Richard I, known as Richard the Lion-Hearted. Though not Henry's choice to become king, Richard was Eleanor's favorite, and she sought to establish him as the heir to her lands in France. This move away from Henry foreshadowed the revolt of Eleanor and her sons against Henry.

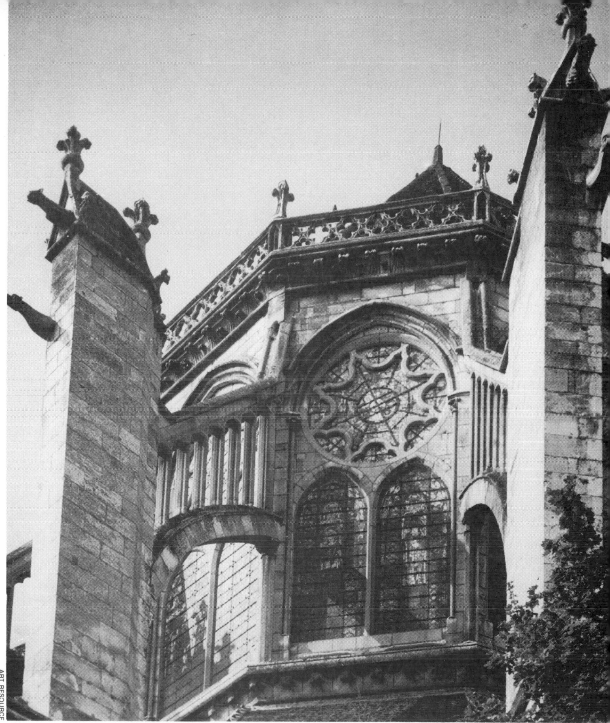

The church of Saint Etienne in Auxerre, France, where Richard was symbolically "married" to St. Valerie of Limoges, a noble virgin martyr. The ceremony, performed as part of Eleanor's efforts to introduce her son to the citizens of Poitou and Aquitaine, advanced Richard's status as the region's rightful heir.

Twelfth-century stained-glass panel with an angel playing a musical instrument. Richard, displaying the artistic talent of Eleanor's family, was reputed to be an accomplished poet and singer in his own right.

Medieval jousting tournament. Such competitions became popular throughout western Europe, and especially with Henry the Young King, as they afforded young nobles a chance to display their military prowess. The object of a joust was not to kill one's opponent (though that often happened) but to unhorse him.

THE BETTMANN ARCHIVE

Henry II, as seen in a 1529 woodcut. In 1173 Eleanor, her sons, and other discontented nobles launched a revolt against the king; however, the insurrection failed and Eleanor was brought back captive to England by Henry. Her imprisonment would last 15 years.

gether to the Middle East. As in the Second Crusade, enormous amounts of money had to be raised all over England and the continent, which was a great hardship on a populace already heavily taxed. Preparations were made and Henry said his goodbyes to Eleanor and to England; it was now his turn to go to the Holy Land at the age of 55. But Henry never got to Jerusalem. In fact, he never set sail from Europe. Richard, Henry's son and heir, had joined forces with Philip Augustus against his father and declared war on him, capturing all of Henry's castles and towns, and forcing Henry and his followers to flee. (John, whom Henry had such trust in and who was with him, dropped out of sight only to turn up in Richard's camp.) Clearly, the old king was being called on to give up his throne, and for months, in the winter and spring of 1188–89, he battled and brooded, finally falling sick in the city of Le Mans, his birthplace.

Historian Kelly states that, "Though worn with pain and utterly depressed by his losses, Henry had not accepted the idea of ultimate defeat." It was his own son Richard who had brought him to this and he cursed him. When he learned of John's defection he was not surprised. On July 6, 1189, Henry of England was dead. He was buried in the abbey of Fontevrault, near Le Mans, where both Richard and Eleanor would one day join him, and it was said that when his son Richard came to pay his last respects, "blood burst from the nostrils of the [dead] king and oozed to the floor." It was as if Henry could not bear to have Richard near him, even in death. Of Henry and the empire he forged, a chronicler wrote,

> This scanty tomb doth now suffice
> For whom the earth was not enough.

It was 1189; soon Richard would be king and Eleanor, after 15 years of imprisonment, was free.

The coronation of Richard I in 1189. The premature death in 1183 of his brother Henry the Young King had left him heir. Richard ascended to the English throne after King Henry died in 1189. He immediately released his mother from her long incarceration.

7

Freedom and Ferment

England's new monarch, Richard, sent one of his most trusted knights to England to free Eleanor from her imprisonment. The 67-year-old queen was already free, however, and many nobles were already making their way to pay homage to her. One historian says that "no one [had] dared to detain her a single hour after news of the king's death had reached England." Moving her household to London at once, convening a court, and gathering in the nobles and high clergy to swear loyalty to their new king, her beloved Richard, Eleanor was very much in control.

Richard had never been fond of England and had spent very little time there. His new subjects thought of him as "a Poitevin," a foreigner. Eleanor's presence made Richard's subjects more willing to accept the new king and the fact that after almost 40 years a new reign was about to begin. She made a grand tour of England, moving from castle to castle, acting on Richard's behalf. She had a general pardon given to all whom Henry had imprisoned, with the condition that those freed should, as Meade observes, "promise to support the government in preserving the peace." She prepared the ground so

She enhanced the grandeur of her birth by the honesty of her life, the purity of her morals, the flower of her virtues; she surpassed almost all the queens of the world.
—Eleanor's obituary, written by the nuns of the Fontevrault Abbey

Richard I, the Lion-Hearted. Richard was said to be the embodiment of the chivalric age — a brave warrior and a sensitive poet-singer at the same time. He ruled as king until 1199, when he was killed while besieging a castle in eastern France.

A manuscript by John of Mandeville showing pilgrims in the Holy Land. Richard was the main force behind the Third Crusade (1191—92). Though his exploits there boosted his prestige, the reconquest of Jerusalem proved impossible, and in 1192 Richard signed a treaty with the powerful Muslim leader, Saladin.

well that when Richard arrived in England, in August 1189, he was welcomed instead of being thought of as the son who had been the cause of his father's death.

Eleanor cleverly managed to show off the new king to the English people in the best and most positive light. Instead of being crowned immediately, as Eleanor and Henry had been 35 years before, Richard and his mother made a leisurely two-week tour through the English countryside. They were warmly welcomed wherever they went. Mother, son, and the entire court came to London for the coronation on September 3. In Richard's honor streets were cleaned and flowers and banners placed everywhere. It is believed that Eleanor herself devised the coronation ceremony, held in London's Westminster Abbey. Much of the ceremony and its trappings has become traditional and has been followed to this day. Three days of general feasting and merrymaking, by nobles and commoners alike, followed Richard's coronation.

Almost immediately after this splendid beginning to his reign, Richard began preparations for a crusade to fulfill the vow taken by his father. His ally, Philip of France, would lead a French army to the Holy Land to fight alongside Richard. Although Henry had been preparing for the venture before he died, new monies had to be raised since all that Henry had accumulated had been spent on his war with Richard and Philip. Richard's methods of obtaining the funds, however, were unscrupulous; he levied taxes cruelly and his new popularity waned. Even his adoring mother had to admit Richard lacked both her political sense and his father's skill for judging character. However, he got his way, as he always seemed to, and the funds were raised. On leaving England, only four months after he was crowned, Richard appointed two regents, a chancellor and a bishop, to act for him and his mother.

From Eleanor, Richard had detailed knowledge of the blunders and misfortunes of the Second Crusade and he was determined not to repeat any of its costly mistakes. He devised strict rules for the Third Crusade: no women were allowed to go along, there

> *She possessed a certain restlessness, a lack of discipline that made it difficult for her to tolerate restrictions, an impatience that did not allow her to suffer boredom easily.*
> —MARION MEADE
> historian, on Eleanor

King Richard as seen in a 1528 woodcut. In 1192, on his way home from the Third Crusade, Richard was kidnapped in Vienna in retribution for his insulting gestures toward Austrian troops during the Holy Land fighting. He was held captive for more than a year until Queen Eleanor arrived in Germany to pay the high ransom.

was to be a well-trained and well-disciplined army, and the expedition was to travel by sea in well-outfitted and well-provisioned ships. His mother, however, had no enthusiasm for the Third Crusade. Knowing from experience how dangerous such a venture could be, she was determined at least to see to it that Richard married and produced an heir as quickly as possible in order to insure the succession before risking his life. With this in mind, she crossed the English Channel to France in February of 1190, for the first time since Henry's death and her release from captivity.

The business of the Plantagenet succession was by now a real problem; all of Henry's empire-building seemed in jeopardy. Young Henry and Geoffrey were dead; Geoffrey's son, Arthur of Brittany, was the only male child on the horizon, but was not in good

Twelfth-century French musicians. It is said that while a prisoner in Austria, Richard used his musical and poetic gifts to compose ballads.

standing with the Plantagenets; John had just recently wed and Richard remained unmarried.

The new king had avoided marriage up to this time, although he had been betrothed for years to the French princess, Alais Capet. Complicated factors, both personal and political, had always delayed the marriage and now it was finally called off. At the age of 33 it was understood that Richard had no interest in women. For a king with a dynasty to preserve, however, that was irrelevant. Eleanor would see to it that a bride whom she considered suitable would be found. Within weeks she had chosen Princess Berengaria of Navarre, a province near the Pyrenees mountains. In the winter of 1191 Eleanor, almost 70 years old, made her way across the icy Alps to Italy. From there she journeyed southward to Messina in Sicily, where the crusading armies were spending the winter, and brought Richard his bride. Because of Eleanor's persistence, the marriage later took place in Cyprus, but the two hardly lived together and the union remained childless.

In July 1191 Richard of England, leading the Third Crusade, set out for the Holy Land. Philip Augustus and his forces had gone ahead. Eleanor, continuing her astonishing travel feats, recrossed the Alps and went to Marseilles, the Mediterranean seaport in southern France, to see her son off. Even before the crusade, Richard the Lion-Hearted was, in Meade's words, "being extolled as the hero of the century, a prince to whom no amount of praise could do justice." He was compared to such great men of the past as Alexander the Great and Odysseus, the hero of Homer's *Odyssey*. In Palestine, Richard's courage in fighting the Muslims was inspirational to all his troops; to this day his name is equated with the highest standards of daring and courage. A story is told that in the Middle East, for many generations after the Third Crusade, Arab women would frighten their children into behaving by telling them that if they were not good, *Malik Ric* (King Richard in Arabic) would get them.

But great heroism invites great envy, and Richard's case was no exception. Philip Augustus, who

> *Eleanor had done her best to personally inaugurate her son's reign with memorable splendor, but despite her exertions to ingratiate her son with his subjects, she could not disguise the fact that Richard regarded [England] as little more than a milk cow for the sustenance of his most important concern, the Crusade to rescue Jerusalem.*
>
> —MARION MEADE
> historian

had been Richard's supporter and ally, first against Henry and now in the crusade, was so jealous of the new king's popularity and success that his friendship turned to bitter enmity. When some Austrian troops, fighting under the banner of the emperor of the Holy Roman Empire, claimed victory at the siege of the city of Acre by flying their flag from the tallest tower, Richard, the commander of the siege, ordered the flag tossed into the mud-packed moat. Such brazen insults mounted until the world's greatest knight was hated as much as he was loved.

Meanwhile, in Europe, Eleanor was maintaining the empire. She handled some political difficulties

But why need we expend labor extolling so great a man? He needs no superfluous commendation. He was superior to all others.
—one of Richard's contemporaries, praising him after his death

A knight in armor from the time of Philip Augustus, 1180. The French king, who had earlier allied with Richard in his revolt against Henry, joined the English monarch in the Third Crusade; however, relations between the two kings grew strained even before they reached the Holy Land.

in the continental territories as well as the overly zealous John, who was trying to get more power for himself in his brother's absence. It was a shock to her when Philip Augustus of France returned from the crusade at the end of 1191, saying that he had been too ill to remain, and leaving Richard to cope with the Muslims alone. The old queen's anxiety for her son was tremendous and it was with great relief

Mural painting of Richard and the Crusaders leaving for the Holy Land. Upon his death Eleanor's lament included the words she had written during his imprisonment: "I have lost the staff of my age, the light of my eyes."

that she finally received the news a year later that, though there had been no real victory any more than in the Second Crusade, a truce had been reached with the Turks and Richard was on his way home. However, in December 1192, Richard was kidnapped near Vienna, the capital of the duchy of Austria, his remembered insults on the crusade being the immediate cause, and was held for a "king's

Eleanor of Aquitaine and her daughter-in-law, Isabella of Angoulême (John's second wife) from a mural dating from the year 1200 in the Chapel of Sainte-Radegonde at Chinon. Since Richard died childless, the Plantagenet inheritance passed to John, who would eventually lose most of the French Angevin territories to Philip Augustus.

ransom"; it was "a price that would bring Plantagenet arrogance to the dust," Kelly states. The ransom was to include a fortune of 100,000 marks of silver — many millions of English pounds in today's money — and hundreds of noble hostages to be sent to insure payment.

Richard of England was held prisoner over a year and was said to have been as gallant and courteous in his captivity as his mother had been in hers. Some of the poems and ballads he wrote during this period survive to this day and show a real gift for verse. During this time his mother, who virtually ruled the Angevin domains alone, taxed everyone throughout the empire, draining every resource. She maintained voluminous correspondence with the Holy Roman emperor and the pope and continued to cope with John's antics (while his mother was laboring to have Richard freed, John was making incursions on his brother's authority by claiming Richard would never return and that he was now as good as king himself). Philip Augustus made matters worse by urging the Holy Roman emperor to make the ransom higher, arguing that more

FROM *ELEANOR OF AQUITAINE* BY DESMOND SWEARD, TIMES BOOKS

money could be obtained for such a prize as the Plantagenet king. Finally, accompanied by many great lords and noble hostages, Queen Eleanor arrived in Germany's Rhine Valley in January 1194 to pay the ransom in person and to be reunited with her precious son without any further delay. But there were difficulties in negotiating the terms of his release, and to Eleanor's dismay it was not until February that the king was liberated. Finally, as Kelly informs us, an exhausted queen "worn with labor and anguish" fell weeping into her son's arms.

Now that Richard was restored, alive and well, to the English throne, Eleanor could relax a little, and for the next few years she spent some needed quiet and restful time at her favorite abbey of Fontevrault near Le Mans, where Henry was buried. For the next few years Richard, "against heavy odds," Kelly points out, "recovered Angevin prestige and comparative security." John was forgiven for having tried to take the throne while Richard was in prison, and Eleanor, apparently, was instrumental in reconciling her two sons. True, the succession was still a problem, but Richard was still comparatively young. Then, in 1199, when Richard was feeling a need to fill his treasury, most of the money he had at the time having been spent on some minor battles with Philip Augustus, some ancient treasure was reported to have been unearthed in one of the many provinces that made up the Angevin domains. Richard, as overlord, laid claim to it and went, with a small group, to take it for himself. While besieging the local castle he was wounded by a crossbow bolt. He lingered for a couple of weeks, but the wound became infected and on April 6, 1199, he died in his mother's arms. Childless, he designated his brother John as his heir to the English throne and all the Plantagenet lands.

Eleanor's grief was enormous. Her favorite child lay dead at 41, all that she had worked and suffered for seemed for naught. She was 77 years old, and of the 10 children to whom she had given birth only two remained; Eleanor, queen of Castile, and John, now king of England.

Eleanor was to know no peace for her remaining

> *Queen Eleanor, a matchless woman, beautiful and chaste, powerful and modest, meek and eloquent which is rarely to be met with in a woman; who was sufficiently advanced in years to have two husbands and two sons crowned kings, still indefatigable for every undertaking, whose power was the admiration of her age . . . .*
> —RICHARD OF DEVIZES
> English chronicler and monk

Eleanor of Aquitaine's tomb site at Fontevrault. As if to symbolize her lifelong devotion to literature and the arts, her figure in effigy holds a book.

five years. John, for whom she tried to do her best as Richard's designated successor, had a great deal of trouble not only with Philip Augustus and the vassals of his continental territories but also with his nephew, Arthur of Brittany, who laid claim to the English throne. Instead of indulging her grief for Richard, Eleanor made a final stand to do what she could to bring about a consolidation of the remains of Henry's empire and to effect a peace between the Capets and the Plantagenets. She personally made a journey to Spain to bring back her granddaughter, Blanche of Castile, to be the bride of Philip's son, the future King Louis VIII. Perhaps then, Eleanor reasoned, the old enmities would be forgotten and a new era for European peace and prosperity could begin.

Nearing 80, Eleanor needed to rest after her diplomatic mission to Spain in 1200. Although she sometimes met with John in Rouen and other Plantagenet cities on family business, she basically remained at the abbey of Fontevrault, where she died in April 1204. It was her final home as well as her final resting place.

Eleanor's life had spanned practically the whole of the 12th century and she had been privileged to experience more of life's possibilities than most people have in any age. She left an enormous legacy, the most lasting aspect of which has been the literary troubadour tradition. C.S. Lewis, the eminent English writer and thinker, has said that the troubadours "effected a change which left no corner of our ethics, our imagination, or our daily life untouched." Of the inspiration behind the great troubadour tradition a contemporary chronicler, Richard of Devizes, wrote: "Queen Eleanor [was] an incomparable woman, whose power was the admiration of her age."

The abbey at Fontevrault, where Eleanor, Henry II, and Richard I are buried. Eleanor spent her final years here, remaining an active player in the continuing disputes between England and France.

111

Further Reading

Barber, Richard. *Henry Plantagenet.* Totawa, N.J.: Rowman & Littlefield, Inc., 1973.

Goldman, James. *The Lion in Winter.* New York: Random House, 1966.

Huizinga, J. *The Waning of the Middle Ages.* London: Edward Arnold, 1937.

Kelly, Amy. *Eleanor of Aquitaine and the Four Kings.* Cambridge: Harvard University Press, 1950.

Magill, Frank A., ed. *Great Events from History (Ancient and Medieval Series),* 951–1500, vol. III. Englewood Cliffs, N.J.: Salem Press, 1972.

Meade, Marion. *Eleanor of Aquitaine.* New York: Hawthorn Books, 1977.

Plaidy, Jean. *The Revolt of the Eaglets.* New York: Fawcett Crest, 1981.

Walker, Curtis Howe. *Eleanor of Aquitaine.* Chapel Hill: University of North Carolina Press, 1950.

Chronology

1122	Eleanor born in Aquitaine, France
1130	Death of Eleanor's mother and brother
April 1137	Death of father, Duke William X; Eleanor becomes duchess of Aquitaine and countess of Poitou
July 25, 1137	Eleanor marries Louis VII of France, becomes queen of France
1145	Birth of first child, Marie Capet
1147–49	Eleanor and Louis take part in the unsuccessful Second Crusade to the Holy Land
Oct. 1149	Pope Eugenius denies Eleanor's request for a divorce
1150	Eleanor gives birth to a second daughter, Alix Capet
1152	Divorces Louis, marries Henry Plantagenet (later Henry II)
1153	Birth of first son, William Plantagenet
Dec. 19, 1154	Eleanor and Henry crowned queen and king of England
1155	Birth of second son, Henry Plantagenet
1156	Birth of Matilda Plantagenet, later duchess of Saxony Death of Prince William
1157	Birth of Richard Plantagenet
1158	Birth of Geoffrey Plantagenet, later count of Brittany
1161	Birth of Eleanor Plantagenet, later queen of Castile
1165	Birth of Joanna Plantagenet, later queen of Sicily
1166	Birth of last child, John Plantagenet
1168	Eleanor leaves Henry and returns to Aquitaine
1169	Establishes the court of love in Poitiers, France
1173	The young Plantagenets, with Eleanor's help, unsuccessfully revolt against King Henry
1174	Henry's men disband the court of love and arrest Eleanor, who is imprisoned in England for the next fifteen years
1183	Henry Plantagenet, the heir to the throne, dies
1186	Geoffrey Plantagenet dies
July 1189	King Henry dies; Eleanor is freed from captivity
Sept. 3, 1189	Richard is crowned King of England
1191	Richard embarks on Third Crusade, Eleanor crosses the Alps to bring him a bride, Berengaria of Navarre
1192	Richard is captured and held for ransom in Vienna, Austria
1194	After Eleanor brings ransom money to Germany, Richard is released
1199	Richard is killed; John becomes king of England
1200	Eleanor crosses the Pyrenees to bring French Crown Prince Louis a bride, her granddaughter, Blanche of Castile
April 1, 1204	Dies in the abbey of Fontevrault

Index

Zoë Coralnik Kaplan is a former actress and producer of educational radio and television shows. She attended London's Royal Academy of Dramatic Art and appeared on stage, television, and radio, both in New York and London. Since receiving her Ph.D. in Theatre and Comparative Literature from the City University of New York, she has been a university professor. In addition to teaching at CUNY, Marymount Manhattan College, and the New School for Social Research, she has published poetry, articles and essays.

Arthur M. Schlesinger, jr., taught history at Harvard for many years and is currently Albert Schweitzer Professor of the Humanities at City University of New York. He is the author of numerous highly praised works in American history and has twice been awarded the Pulitzer Prize. He served in the White House as special assistant to Presidents Kennedy and Johnson.